19TH CENTURY
LUSTREWARE

Frontispiece. *A pink lustre moulded jug, c.1825. (See Colour Plate 129, page 134)*

Title page. *A silver resist lustre teapot, c.1820s. (See Colour Plate 145, page 157)*

19TH CENTURY LUSTREWARE

Michael Gibson

ANTIQUE COLLECTORS' CLUB

ISBN 1 85149 306 9

British Library Cataloguing-in-Publication Data
A catalogue record for this book is available from the British Library

Printed in England
by the Antique Collectors' Club Ltd., Woodbridge, Suffolk
on Consort Royal Satin paper
supplied by the Donside Paper Company, Aberdeen, Scotland

ANTIQUE COLLECTORS' CLUB

THE ANTIQUE COLLECTORS' CLUB was formed in 1966 and quickly grew to a five figure membership spread throughout the world. It publishes the only independently run monthly antiques magazine, *Antique Collecting*, which caters for those collectors who are interested in widening their knowledge of antiques, both by greater awareness of quality and by discussion of the factors which influence the price that is likely to be asked. The Antique Collectors' Club pioneered the provision of information on prices for collectors and the magazine still leads in the provision of detailed articles on a variety of subjects.

It was in response to the enormous demand for information on 'what to pay' that the price guide series was introduced in 1968 with the first edition of *The Price Guide to Antique Furniture* (completely revised 1978 and 1989), a book which broke new ground by illustrating the more common types of antique furniture, the sort that collectors could buy in shops and at auctions rather than the rare museum pieces which had previously been used (and still to a large extent are used) to make up the limited amount of illustrations in books published by commercial publishers. Many other price guides have followed, all copiously illustrated, and greatly appreciated by collectors for the valuable information they contain, quite apart from prices. The Price Guide Series heralded the publication of many standard works of reference on art and antiques. *The Dictionary of British Art* (now in six volumes), *The Pictorial Dictionary of British 19th Century Furniture Design*, *Oak Furniture* and *Early English Clocks* were followed by many deeply researched reference works such as *The Directory of Gold and Silversmiths*, providing new information. Many of these books are now accepted as the standard work of reference on their subject.

The Antique Collectors' Club has widened its list to include books on gardens and architecture. All the Club's publications are available through bookshops world wide and a full catalogue of all these titles is available free of charge from the addresses below.

Club membership, open to all collectors, costs little. Members receive free of charge *Antique Collecting*, the Club's magazine (published ten times a year), which contains well-illustrated articles dealing with the practical aspects of collecting not normally dealt with by magazines. Prices, features of value, investment potential, fakes and forgeries are all given prominence in the magazine.

Among other facilities available to members are private buying and selling facilities and the opportunity to meet other collectors at their local antique collectors' club. There are over eighty in Britain and more than a dozen overseas. Members may also buy the Club's publications at special pre-publication prices.

As its motto implies, the Club is an organisation designed to help collectors get the most out of their hobby: it is informal and friendly and gives enormous enjoyment to all concerned.

For Collectors — By Collectors — About Collecting

ANTIQUE COLLECTORS' CLUB
5 Church Street, Woodbridge Suffolk IP12 1DS, UK
Tel: 01394 385501 Fax: 01394 384434
or
Market Street Industrial Park, Wappingers' Falls, NY 12590, USA
Tel: 914 297 0003 Fax: 914 297 0068

The top, right-hand pink lustre wall plaque features a moulded figure of an Entertainer, picked out in red, puce, blue, green and black enamels, and is a considerable rarity, possibly of Sunderland origin, c.1830. Ht 6⅛in: 157mm. It makes a pair with the second wall plaque, which depicts a jester and is marginally larger at 6½in: 165mm. (Sotheby's)

ACKNOWLEDGEMENTS AND THANKS

I should like to thank all the people and institutions which have provided a number of the illustrations, both black and white and in colour, which appear in this book. They are individually named, where they wish it, as a part of the captions. Others, with the security of their collections in mind, have preferred to remain anonymous. Those who have been especially helpful include Mr and Mrs Arthur J. Gutman of Baltimore, who have allowed me to use many pictures of lustreware from their remarkable collection on the other side of the Atlantic. Most of the black and white photographs of their pieces were taken by John Harbold. Some of the other pictures are from the collection of Mr and Mrs J.J. Robinson.

Messrs Sotheby's, through Christina Donaldson of their Ceramics Department, have also been especially helpful and generous in the provision of pictures.

My wife and I are equal partners in the research that goes into a book of this kind, and her contribution to the final preparation of the manuscript has been immense. However, my warmest appreciation must, I think, be reserved for Harold and Clarice Blakey. I have imposed quite shamelessly on their enthusiasm, good nature and vast knowledge in seeking help in areas where my own knowledge was, perhaps, rather scanty. Their response was always immediate and comprehensive, as one would expect from the ex-Editors of the *Northern Ceramic Society's Newsletter.*

A pair of pearlware purple lustre flat-back bulb pots with covers, that on the left with a fairly conventional 'cottage' style decoration, and a huntsman and hounds in a landscape *on the other. Probably Staffordshire, c.1825. Width 8¼in: 210mm.* *(Sotheby's)*

CONTENTS

A rare pair of pink lustre memorial wall plaques to two members of one family, Robert Moor Bishop and Betsy Susan Bishop, giving the dates of their births and deaths. Betsy Susan was less than one year old. Either Sunderland or Staffordshire. Width 6½in: 165mm.

(Sotheby's)

INTRODUCTION

A great many people, when asked if they would like to see our lustre collection, take on a rather hesitant expression, saying quite clearly that they do not know what we are talking about. The simplest explanation, that lustreware consists of a ceramic object with a thin, metallic film applied to its surface for decoration, makes it sound like something from the Christmas tree.

Other people, asked the same question, tell us that they think their grandmother had some lustre and that it is probably in the cupboard under the stairs. Produced, it almost inevitably turns out to be a rather tired-looking copper lustre milk jug.

But neither of these instances compares with that of a distant cousin of my wife's visiting us for the first time, someone to whom even the finest cup and saucer would be purely for drinking tea, and who was asked the same question. Actually seeing it rendered him speechless, though not, I suspect, from admiration. My wife, anxious to help him over an awkward silence said: 'Of course we know that not everybody likes lustre', at which he put his foot well and truly in it by replying: 'Well, as long as *you* like it, that's the main thing!'

Old copper lustre items, a great many of which have survived because of their popularity in the nineteenth century and the consequent vast numbers in which they were produced, have a good deal to do with the lack of popular knowledge about just how varied the range of lustreware really is. Copper is what one principally sees around and, while it can be most attractive in itself, particularly in combination with enamels and coloured slips, it is only part of the range. It is in the silver, pink and purple lustre that the real attraction and real quality is to be found. And it is by no means scarce.

The majority of lustreware was made for everyday use and ranges from folk art that became so popular that it achieved mass-production figures at the less expensive end of the market, to pieces of the utmost sophistication and great beauty, clearly intended for the show case rather than the kitchen dresser. My hope is that this book will help to show how much beauty there is waiting for the uninitiated to discover.

CHAPTER I

Lustreware and its Early History

Lustreware is not a type of pottery in the sense that creamware, pearlware or, indeed, the various types of china wares are. Lustre is a form of decoration which can be applied to any form of ceramic body, be it earthenware or porcelain.

Basically there are two forms of lustring. The first, and earliest historically, is the Hispano-Moresque or iridescent lustre, based on ancient techniques originating in the Middle East, in which the lustre is incorporated in the glaze, resulting in all kinds of striking (though not always predictable) effects after it is fired. Quite a few firms in the United Kingdom used it commercially, among them Malings of Newcastle, Pilkingtons (The Royal Lancastrian Pottery) and Wedgwood, but nowadays it is more or less confined to the studio potters. These are not generally looking for uniformity of decoration, even within one set of jugs, bowls or whatever it may be, so for them its unpredictability is a bonus.

In the second form of lustre decoration, the one with which this book is principally concerned, the decorative design is formed from metal, dissolved in acid and applied as a thin film on top of the glaze, either with a brush or in certain cases by dipping. It is then fired, reducing the oxidised metal in the lustre solution to its original metallic form. Often it was used in combination with sprigging and enamel colours.

During the second half of the eighteenth century and the very early years of the nineteenth century, before the discovery of this second lustring process, many not very successful attempts were made to apply a variety of metallic finishes to ceramics in order to give them novelty and an extra sparkle. Gilding was, of course, well established, but it was quite a labour intensive process, involving as it did first the application of the gold and then burnishing. This made it relatively expensive but, while the two metals principally used in lustring were again gold and also platinum, the quantity needed to make up the thin metallic film was so minute that the process could be used economically on even the humblest wares.

Gold, when used in lustring, resulted in such a thin film

Colour Plate 1. *This Spode cup and saucer and coffee can, decorated with gilding and a broad band of silver lustre, is one of the very earliest examples of the art of lustring. It is even possible that it may have been decorated in the* Daniel workshops by John Hancock himself. The lustre has that 'steely' look, characteristic of much of the earliest work. c.1805.

that all trace of the golden colour was lost. If used on a light coloured background, it appeared as a pink sheen, two or more coatings or the addition of a small amount of tin to

Plate 2. *A 'Tyneside School' marriage jug with a Masonic decorative theme and the typical brown enamel sprigs of leaves and corn ears of the middle period, c.1828-1830. Ht 8in: 205mm. See also Colour Plate 120.*

(Sotheby's)

the mixture gradually deepening the tone until it became purple lustre. On brown clay pottery or pottery with a dark slip the gold lustre took on a copper hue, creating the well-known copper lustre. This changed to something more nearly resembling gold if the lustre was used over an orange slip, as is done in some modern reproductions. Copper itself was used experimentally early on but was found to produce a dull and sometimes spotty effect. In the same way, real silver was originally tried to produce silver lustre, but it resulted in a rather dull finish which, before long, tarnished. Polishing such a thin coating of metal was hardly to be recommended as it would very soon have worn it away. Platinum, which came into commercial production towards the end of the eighteenth century, was found to be a more than satisfactory substitute, retaining its brightness and quite untarnishable.

Many of the designs, using the lustre mixture applied freehand with a brush (known as a pencil), were so simple that they could be carried out by children once they had been given a pattern to copy. As in so many industries in the 1800s, the use of child labour in the potteries resulted in a great saving in wages. A pictorial theme they could easily cope with, making it a universal favourite with manufacturers (and, it must be admitted, with customers, too), was the 'primitive' or 'cottage' decoration. This generally showed a rural scene with trees and a building of some sort and as a rule pink lustre was used for it. Often thought of as exclusively coming from Sunderland,

Colour Plate 2. *A handsome and very practical porcelain pink lustre teapot without, as many of them had, too many ceramic flights of fancy in the form of knobs and curlicues that were very easily broken in everyday use. Probably Staffordshire, c.1820s. Ht 6½in: 166mm.*

'cottage'-style decoration was also carried out in just about every ceramic centre in the north of England, in Wales, and by the Scottish potteries. There is a tendency nowadays to ascribe almost any kind of lustre to Sunderland under the heading of Sunderland Ware, and this applies even when the lustre decoration is on porcelain, which the many Sunderland potteries never produced (though it is true that, in the later period, a small proportion of the output of the Wear Valley was made up of porcelain blanks imported from Staffordshire for decoration. However, the amount was never significant).

Silver resist lustre is another type over which there is confusion. To many people all silver lustre is resist, though the resist technique is used only on certain pieces, as will be described in Chapter 2.

Once the lustring process was truly launched in Staffordshire, in 1805, its popularity spread very rapidly. It was to become in time a major industry with a huge export market, especially to the continent of Europe and to America, but was almost entirely confined to potteries in the northern half of the United Kingdom. As a result, many of the northern potteries found it worth their while to set up London warehouses or retail shops, and also agencies abroad. Lustre became especially popular in France, where it was, and still is, known as Jersey Ware, being imported through Jersey, one of the Channel Islands. A lot was also bought by foreign sailors as souvenirs of their visits to the United Kingdom, especially from the potteries

of the north-east, the lustre-producing centres of Sunderland and Newcastle and Stockton all being thriving seaports as, indeed, was Liverpool in the west, which served, with Hull, as an outlet for the Staffordshire wares. Considerable collections of lustreware are still to be found in Holland and the Scandinavian countries, enough for a book, *Sailor Souvenirs,* to be written about them by Dr Wolfgang Rudolph. He has this to say: 'A count of all the pieces with a manufacturer's mark in the combined collections of the regional maritime museums of Rugen, Hidensee, Zingst, Prerow and Warnemunde with the additional specimens of nine private collections – all of which items came from sailors' households…showed that 260 out of 650 or a total of 40% came from factories in Yorkshire, Northumberland and Scotland. If it were possible to include lustreware items (which are almost without exception unsigned), the average of goods imported by individual crewmen originating in the northern coastal region would be certain to be much higher'. It is here worth making the point that museums tend to go for marked pieces and, as the north-eastern potteries marked more frequently than most, it is not surprising that they were better represented, though the general point Dr Rudolph is making is valid.

The use of transfer printing in combination with lustre must have made a considerable difference to the export trade, for it was possible for transfers to be designed for specific markets. Views of foreign cities or well-known

Plate 3. *A fine pair of presentation creamware pink lustre jugs with most unusual 'strap' handles. The ship on the right-hand jug is painted in light* green enamel. Probably Staffordshire c.1820-30. Hts 7in: 178mm.
(Tolson Collection)

monuments and buildings appealed to the nationals of the countries in which the cities were situated. Leading statesmen and other notabilities, military as well as political, would also be featured and, for the American market, Staffordshire and possibly Liverpool (the former exporting, as has just been said, through the latter) produced topical designs featuring prize fighters and other leading U.S. sportsmen. It is an interesting sidelight on the commercial practices of the time that some of these came in very useful when pottery transfer designs were needed later to feature

Plate 4. *Silver resist jug with a very appealing owl in bright enamel colours in the reserve. Probably Staffordshire, c.1830.* (Gutman Collection).

a character in the news on this side of the Atlantic for they could be re-used. There is, for instance, a lustre jug that was in the Baker Collection captioned Hunt and Liberty and purporting to show Henry Hunt who was involved in the notorious Peterloo Reform meeting in Manchester in 1819, but which is, in fact, a portrait of Commodore Bainbridge of the United States Navy. There were no news photographs or television in those days to show what the people really looked like, so any old picture would do! John and Baker's *Old English Lustre Pottery* gives a very full coverage of Staffordshire wares exported to America.

Transfer designs were, as will be seen, widely used in combination with lustre for the home market as well. The Sunderland jugs are perhaps the best known examples of this with their prints of the Wear Bridge (Sunderland is on the river Wear) based on over forty different engravings. These could be considered their trademark if it were not for the fact that the Wear Bridge print can also be found on pieces from neighbouring Newcastle upon Tyne and even on jugs from Stockton-on-Tees, much further down the coast to the south. The reasons for this are readily explained, if not excused, for when a pottery went out of business, its equipment, which included the expensive copper printing plates for the transfers, was usually bought by another firm. They would be re-used by them even, in some cases, when they had the name of the original owner worked into the design, for there were no laws then to prevent this. Not only transfer prints but any decorative design that proved popular would be blatantly copied by all and sundry, thus contributing greatly to the problems experienced nowadays in establishing who produced what.

Only in one case can the use of the Sunderland Bridge motif by both Sunderland and Newcastle be really excused, and that was when Robert Maling moved his pottery business from Sunderland to Newcastle upon Tyne. One could hardly expect him to scrap his most popular printing plates and he continued producing jugs and other things featuring the Wear Bridge. Transfer prints were, of course, used in all the ceramic centres that produced lustre and some examples of these are discussed more fully in Chapter 2.

Potentially most potteries in the north of England (and in Scotland and Wales too) may have tried out the new and exciting lustre decoration. Some, for one reason or another, dropped it, others continued with a limited production, while yet others made lustred wares one of their most important products. Some specialists in lustring used it on their own wares, and also carried it out for others. Yet others, even more specialist, were not potters but lustre decorators only, again carrying out decorating work for many factories. Since very few of the lustred pieces from any of these sources, either pottery or porcelain, were marked, this practice adds to the difficulty, already pretty mountainous, of identifying origins – not that this should be

Plate 5. *A typical scene in the Potteries in the 19th century showing the Churchyard Works, Burslem, owned by the Wedgwood family for several generations. The inevitable pot ovens dominate the skyline.*

allowed to deter a collector, for if one searches hard enough, talks to enough fellow collectors and lustre dealers and visits enough museums, clues do begin to emerge. Comparisons can be made with known marked pieces of a distinctive design, or a jug with no lustre in the decoration but from a known factory may help to place a nearly identical lustred one. Lustreware is great fun to collect simply because it came from so many sources. One never knows what to expect next and it can range from the cheap and rather mundane to pieces of exquisite workmanship. Colours can be beautifully blended, but are often bright, not to say gaudy, and certain pieces will be found to have the happy vulgarity of the Victorian music hall, with which many of them were, of course, contemporary. Somehow, however, they all seem to blend together into one harmonious whole.

Because so much lustreware was produced there is still plenty of it about, which is encouraging for the collector though, as a large proportion of lustre decoration was carried out on wares made to be used and not simply for the display cabinet, a good many pieces, especially those in earthenware, will be chipped or cracked. The extent of this damage will determine the price, cracks being considered more serious than a few minor chips.

Prices, even for the better pieces, though rising like those of everything else, are still low in comparison with those of their equivalents in porcelain. They are still within reach of the more modest collector. Lustre decoration on porcelain as opposed to pottery is in rather a different category and prices will be higher.

As mentioned earlier, many attempts were made towards the end of the eighteenth century and the beginning of the nineteenth to find a way to give ceramics a metallic finish. This finish did not necessarily have to be over-all coverage, but was often in the form of banding or other decoration which would point up and add sparkle to what might otherwise be a rather sombre piece of ware. An over-all

Plate 6. *A copper lustre jug, c.1820-30, fitted with a feature not too often seen on lustreware, a hinged Britannia metal lid impressed with the name of B. Grayson and Son, Sheffield. The floral sprigging is in mixed enamel colours. Ht 5in: 127mm.*

Colour Plate 3. *These oval section moulded jugs are typical of the pink lustreware put out by many Staffordshire potteries and some other areas in the 1820s. On the reverse the left-hand one has, in relief, one of the favourite decorative themes – putti romping with a goat. The side shown here is much more unusual, with its three, square-rigged ships in full sail under a cloudy sky. The other jug has a more familiar sporting theme. Hts 6in: 152mm.*

Plate 7. *A mixed bag of Staffordshire spill vases. The pair at the back, with fluted rims, is in silver resist lustre and probably of a comparatively late date (c.1860-70). The central one is the most unusual in design, moulded in pearlware and with boldly-drawn floral transfer prints in black and copper lustre banding. The second pair combines copper lustre bases and banding and coloured transfer prints, each one different. c.1820-30.*

metallic finish might, however, be used if a ceramic statuette was to be made to look as if it was cast from bronze or silver. So coated, it could be manufactured for a fraction of what it would have cost if cast from the actual metal. Ceramic writer Robin Reilly tells us '…ornamenting earthenware with an encaustic gold bronze…In applying the bronze powder, grind some of it in oil of turpentine and apply this by sponge to the vessel finished, ready for burning, but not quite dry, polish it; heat the ware as is necessary for it; afterwards burnish the bronze.' Bronze and silver both needed burnishing and later polishing if they were to remain bright, which was a good deal of trouble, but in addition the finely abrasive polishes available at the time would all too soon wear away the metal. It was also difficult to avoid staining the uncoated pottery sections.

A more general practice was to present ceramic pieces in silver, gold or silver-gilt mounts and some magnificent examples are known, many of them dating into the eighteenth century or earlier. Jugs might also be given silver or old Sheffield plate rims, lids or handles, though in the case of stonewares the mounts or rims might be, on rare occasions, in a pewter alloy.

Running in parallel with these developments were the trial and error experiments by a number of potters to see if there was another way forward. This supplemented the researches already going on, at least in the more important potteries, into the basic materials they used, which consisted of continuing trials to see the effect of different additives to the potting clays, to find a whiter white, a greater strength, improved firing qualities, greater translucency in porcelains and all the other desirable qualities. Many different glazes were also tried and, for most of these investigations, a knowledge of the properties of the materials used was almost essential. Men such as Josiah Wedgwood were leaders in employing the scientific approach, though in the case of lustre decoration this came after his death in 1795 and his company was not the first to find the answer.

Much of the pioneer work on what came to be regarded as a very English form of decoration was carried out on the Continent although, once the process of lustring had been mastered, little use was made of it there. One of the first indications of progress came when, in the winter of 1788-9, a distinguished German chemist, Martin Heinrich Klaproth, consultant to the Royal Berlin Porcelain factory, read a paper to the Berlin Academy under the title 'On the Use of Platina in the Decoration of Porcelain'. Platina was, of course, platinum, the material in which most of the early lustring was carried out. There is, in the Victoria and Albert Museum collection, a statuette of the Greek god, Castor,

Colour Plate 4. *This rather strange, 'cricket stumps' moulding, decorated in pink lustre, was surprisingly popular on jugs from Staffordshire, c.1820, though the maker is unknown. Ht 5in: 127mm. See Colour Plate 89.*

reputed to be of German origin and on which there is platinum lustre decoration, though whether or not it was actually made in the Royal Berlin factory is uncertain. Klaproth's paper was obviously the result of experimental work over a considerable period, during which it is believed that work more or less in parallel was going on at Sèvres in France and also in Vienna.

Plate 8. *A moulded cream jug with a buff-yellow body and the high spots of the moulding picked out in copper lustre. Probably Staffordshire, c.1820s.*

Plate 9. *A Staffordshire bone china sucrier or sugar box with pink lustre decoration. c.1840.*

Sir, In the notice of the death of Mr John Booth, of Well Street, inserted in your last week's paper, it is stated that he was the inventor of lustre for earthenware. I beg to state that this is incorrect, as I was the original inventor of lustre, which is recorded in several works on Potting, and I first put it into practice at Mr. Spode's Manufactury, for Messrs Daniel and Brown, and continued to make it long before either Mr Booth or any other person attempted to do so. If Mr Booth's friends should doubt the truth of this statement, I shall be very happy to furnish them with proof on the subject, or answer any questions which they may think proper. Perhaps Mr Booth's friends are not aware that I am still alive, although at the advanced age of 89. By inserting this you will oblige one whose character is at stake.
John Hancock
Etruria.

John Hancock was a well-respected decorator of porcelain and earthenware who, though born in Nottingham, was first apprenticed to William Duesbury, owner of the Derby porcelain works from 1756 to 1786. An important figure in the ceramic industry, Duesbury also took over the Bow factory from 1760 and added Chelsea to his stable in 1770. Hancock could hardly have found a better place to learn his craft than Derby, with its highly skilled decorators and finest of porcelains. It was there that he began his experimentation with the use of enamel colours, which showed that he had an enquiring mind and was ever on the lookout for something that would enhance still further the product on which he worked.

About the middle of the 1780s he had moved on and was employed by William and John Turner of Lane End in the Staffordshire potteries. Quite where and when he carried out his research into the craft of lustring, and whether or not he had some access to information from the continental potters as a base from which to work, is not known, but in one way or another he certainly mastered it. At the time he claimed to have introduced it he was working, as his letter states, for Messrs Daniel and Brown, a firm of independent decorators who were under contract to 'Mr Spode's manufactury' and actually worked within their premises. In other words, he was now producing work for the famous firm established in 1776 by the first Josiah Spode, friend and great rival of Josiah Wedgwood I.

1816 saw Hancock move on once more, this time to Etruria and the firm of Josiah Wedgwood II, taking up the position of chief colour-maker and manager of the enamelling department. Although it is fairly certain that Wedgwood were making lustre by the time he arrived, it is likely that, as chief colour-maker, he would have played a major part in the production of their early lustred wares.

John Hancock does seem nowadays to be generally accepted as the introducer of lustreware in England, though this does not mean that there were no other candidates,

It must be assumed that the leading English potters can hardly have been unaware of what was happening across the Channel as they were themselves delving into the mysteries of the new processes. There is, however, no real record of the work they were doing, and what progress was being made. The first known mention of lustring occurs in the Daniel family papers with this entry in Henry Daniel's colour book: 'November 11th 1805, half pound of platina entered by the name pail [pale] gold in Mr S— [Spode's] book.' This ties in, of course, with the two quotes given below from the *Staffordshire Mercury and Potteries Gazette,* the first dated 17 January 1846. They must by now be rather familiar to any student of the history of lustre, for they are always repeated when the subject comes up, but they are such important clues in the over-all story that readers must be patient if they are quoted yet again here. The first is from an obituary.

> On the 11th inst., Mr John Booth, of Nelson Cottage, Well Street, Hanley, in his 82nd year. He was the youngest son of George Booth of Longton Hall, the first manufacturer of china in the Staffordshire Potteries. The deceased was also the inventor of lustre for earthenwares.

Nowadays students of ceramic history will not accept the first part of the claim, but the second is much more interesting in that it could have been within the realms of possibility. However, it provoked a swift response in the form of a letter published in the same paper the following Saturday. This read:

apart, that is, from John Booth. The obituary of John Aynsley, for instance, who lived from 1752 to 1829, claimed he was 'one of the first manufacturers of porcelain in Lane End and the first lusterer', while Simeon Shaw, that not always too accurate nineteenth century historian of the Staffordshire potteries, puts in the claim that it was Hancock, in partnership with William Henning, who was responsible for launching gold and copper lustring in 1823 at the Wolfe factory in Stoke-on-Trent, though there seems to be no other indication that Hancock ever worked for Wolfe. Shaw can also be quoted as saying 'The first maker of silver lustre properly so called, was Mr John Gardener, (now employed by J. Spode, Esq.)'.

A number of more modern writers have made other, always conflicting, claims, some even dating the introduction of lustre quite a long way back into the eighteenth century. If I may quote just one, from an encyclopedia of antiques which with considerable generosity I will not name, published by a very reputable firm; 'Lustreware was introduced in Sunderland in 1770.' Wrong place; wrong century!

Probably the truth is that quite a number of people were on the verge of a breakthrough at the beginning of the nineteenth century and we shall never really know just who was the first. On balance, John Hancock gets the vote and, working where he did and with the commercial backing of the Daniels and the Spode organisation, he was in a very good position to get the new process rapidly into commercial production. To back up his claim, Colour Plate 1 shows a Spode bone china cup and saucer and coffee can, c.1806-7, with broad silver lustre banding in addition to gilding and other decoration. The lustre may be a little dull by later standards, having more the appearance of steel, but this is not an uncommon fault in early pieces due probably to impurities

Plate 10. *The Ivy House works in the centre of Burslem, belonging to John and Thomas Wedgwood. The ivy on the walls of the cottage, from which it took its name, can be clearly seen in this old print.*

in the platinum. It is not, I am sure, as has been claimed by some, because a second application of lustre is needed to achieve full brightness. It certainly is not, at least on a white body, though Thomas Lakin held that two coats were needed on a brown body. Hancock, it appears, claimed the secret of lustring to be his own property and not that of his employers, who would almost certainly have considered it exclusive to themselves and not to be passed on to others. His commercial horizons were more limited, however, and, according to Simeon Shaw, he sold the recipes for the

Plates 11 and 12. *A lustre jug that combines lively decoration with a social document, its two sides showing fashionable transport by the forerunner of the bicycle round about 1820. The legends beneath the coloured transfer prints are,* left, 'THE LADIES' ACCELERATOR' *and,* right, 'A Lift from RICHMOND to CARLTON HOUSE'. *The machine, known as a 'Dandy Horse', was patented in London and Paris in 1818.*

Colour Plate 5. *An oval section pink lustre jug clearly, by the moulding of a goat and putti (on both sides), from the same maker as the jug in Colour* Plate 3, which has this moulding on the reverse. Staffordshire, c.1820. Ht 4¾in: 121mm.

mixtures he used quite freely to rivals in the trade 'for a small sum of money'. Perhaps there were bills to pay.

Gold followed swiftly on the heels of platinum as a metal used for lustre work, giving, as we have seen, a far wider range of decorative effects, ranging from pink to copper. But once again evidence pinpointing its first user is hard to come by. There are conflicting accounts, including the Shaw reference to Hancock above, but pretty strong evidence is contained in an entry in the Daniel notebook late in 1805. It reads: 'Mix well-made starch and a strong solution of gold equal parts - makes a pink lustre on china - works well with a pencil same as Hancock used for the Sphinx candle-stick. To take it out use a soft oil and wash out with turpentine.' But back we come to John Hancock, so that Shaw may have been right.

Due to what many would describe as Hancock's lack of business acumen in distributing his recipes so freely, the use of lustre decoration spread with great rapidity throughout the Potteries. It had the excitement of something really new with infinite possibilities which ceramic decorators everywhere were not slow to appreciate.

The Staffordshire ceramic industry, of course, was not alone in this. By 1807, the Cambrian Pottery (Swansea) was advertising 'Ware ornamented with an entire new Gold Lustre.' This quote is from a trade card put out by their warehouse in Fleet Street, London, which handled Swansea's London sales, and which is now in the Banks Collection in the Department of Prints and Drawings in the British Museum. Lustre seems to have been established in the north-eastern potteries of Sunderland and Newcastle by 1815, and in Leeds and the other Yorkshire potteries, in Liverpool and the many lesser centres perhaps a little earlier.

A point perhaps worth making in this brief review of the early history of lustreware is that towns like Sunderland, Newcastle, Leeds or Swansea, places that figure largely in the story, were not as we know them today. They were relatively small and some did not even exist. They came into being later by the bringing together of neighbouring but quite separate pottery-making small townships or large villages, like the Six Towns (not five, as Arnold Bennett had it) in Staffordshire that became Stoke-on-Trent. Sunderland as an entity came about in the same way and the shaping of both communities will be gone into in more detail in Chapters 4 and 5.

CHAPTER II

Decorating with Lustre

Perhaps it would be as well at this stage to point out that any item that has lustre decoration, either in pottery or porcelain, be it only a lustre rim on a cup, is considered to be lustreware.

Quite a wide range of metals was tried out for use as a lustre coating during the early days before platinum and gold proved to be the best. Iron, silver and copper (as opposed to the copper effect obtained from gold on a dark ground) were among these, and at least one out of this

group continued to be used to a limited extent. Iron oxide produced the yellowish-apricot lustre that is found on quite a number of wares from the factories of the north-east, perhaps mainly those of Ball Brothers of Sunderland and John Carr & Sons of Newcastle. The Moore pottery of Sunderland also used it, as did such Scottish firms as John and Matthew Bell's Glasgow Pottery. Steel and real silver were discarded after platinum appeared because of the rather dull finish they produced and the latter was, of

Colour Plate 6. *An example of how effective simplicity of design can be, combining a blue slip band, narrower copper lustre banding, and a nicely-moulded sprigging of a flower bowl in white applied to each side. Probably Staffordshire, c.1830. Ht 7in: 178mm.*

Plate 13. *A Sunderland plaque with a mottled pink lustre border and a transfer print with a farming theme. On the banner are the words 'God Speed the Plough' and the shield depicts a hay fork and scythe, a sickle and hook, a butter churn and harrow and a plough.*
(Tom More Collection)

course, likely to tarnish. Real copper was tried from time to time until quite late on in the nineteenth century, but it did not produce anything like the brilliance of the best produced from gold. Its finish was not only rather dull and dingy, but was liable to spotting. Thus it was always confined to the very cheapest items and not used by any of the leading factories. Poor firing was also responsible for some pretty dire results when the copper lustred ware looked more as if it were covered in brown paint and had no sheen at all.

We are lucky in that recipes for the preparation of lustre survive from the early days. There were a large number of these, for many of the potteries concerned produced their own variant of what might be called the basic recipe. Each added a little bit of this or a little bit of that to try to steal a march on its rivals with a better, not to say brighter, result. The few examples given below, which came early on and were much copied, should be sufficient for the purpose of a general explanation of the process.

One of the earliest potters who was also a specialist in lustring was Thomas Lakin. In the last part of the eighteenth century he traded as Lakin and Poole and later under his own name only, subsequently joining the firm of John Davenport as manager of the glass works, where he was probably what we now call 'works chemist' and became familiar with the lustring process. After that he once more set up with a partner as an independent decorator. It was during the period 1810-1817 that he produced his own lustreware. He finished his career with

the Leeds Pottery, a firm that produced some of the best lustreware of all. He did not introduce lustre to Leeds, but no doubt the firm drew on his wide experience when he joined them.

When Lakin died, his widow found that she was not particularly well provided for and, to make ends meet, she published and sold on subscription at five guineas a time material her husband had already assembled relating to the whole technology of pottery and porcelain manufacture. From this we will take two of his formulae that relate specifically to lustre. The aqua regia specified in the recipes was a combination of hydrochloric and nitric acid. Process 102 reads:

To make Gold Lustre
Take grain gold and dissolve it in aqua regia…provided the acids are pure, the solution will be readily effected without the assistance of heat. In this solution of gold it will be necessary to add a small portion of grain tin, viz. to 5 dwts of gold in solution, let 5 grains of tin be added; an effervescence takes place when the solution is completed and in a proper condition to be mixed with balsam of sulphur, &c. Take balsam of sulphur 3 parts, spirits of turpentine 2 parts, mix them well together over a slow fire, the affinity which exists between the balsam and turpentine will soon make the whole incorporate, then gradually drop the solution of gold into the menstruum, and keep stirring it all the time until the whole solution be added; provided this mixture should appear too thick, add more turpentine until

a proper consistency takes place, this will be correctly ascertained by observation and experiment. One ounce of gold dissolved in the manner described will make upwards of two pounds weight of prepared lustre, and must be used with turpentine, for all other spirits are injurious.

The turpentine was to give the mixture volatility when it was fired. Lakin's recipe for silver lustre read as follows:

To make Silver or Steel Lustre

The silver lustre or steel lustre, as it is sometimes called, is prepared by taking platina and dissolving it in aqua regia composed of equal parts of spirit of nitre and muriatic acid. The solution does not take place with rapidity, and is with difficulty obtained; therefore, to surmount this obstacle, let the vessel be placed in a sand bath, at a moderate temperature of heat, when the solution will be effected; then take three parts of spirits of tar, and one part of the solution of platina, mixing the solution with the tar very gradually, for as soon as the combination takes place, an effervescence will arise, the nitreous acid will evaporate and leave the platina in combination with the tar. After the above process has been performed, should the menstruum be found too thin and incapable of using, set it in a sand bath as before for a few hours; the spirit of tar will evaporate, and by that means of a proper consistence will be obtained. It must be used with spirits of tar, as all other spirits would be destructive.

The spirits of tar in this case took the place of the turpentine in the first recipe, though why the difference we do not know. These two samples can be taken as typical.

Lustre was always applied to a pot over the glaze, for it had to be fired at a much lower temperature. For the same

Plate 14. *A Staffordshire loving cup, combining copper lustre with mottled pink lustre banding. The copper lustre has additional decoration in the form of dark blue and green enamel flowers. c.1830. Ht 5in: 127mm.*

reason, if there were other forms of decoration – enamels, perhaps – as well as lustre, the lustre was always the last to go on, though the enamel itself had a lower firing temperature than the glaze. The following recipe for iron lustre is quoted from the late Una des Fontaines, author of *Wedgwood Fairyland Lustre*. Iron lustre went by a number of names, yellow, orange, apricot and bronze among them.

Bronze Lustre. Two oz. of Horse Shoe nails, dissolved in

Plate 15. *Typical Staffordshire jugs of the 1820s, showing two of the ways in which copper lustre was used. One combines over-all copper with white sprigging and the other, with a blue body, has copper lustre in a broad band round the neck and covering the handle. The rather unusual decoration in the reserve is not a transfer print but painted in pink lustre.*

Colour Plates 7 and 8. *A pink lustre plate and dish showing completely different decorative styles, each attractive in its own way. The yellow-breasted* bird *appears on a variety of lustred pieces. Both unmarked but probably Staffordshire, c.1820s, and both 8in: 203mm in diameter.*

Colour Plate 9. *A very large (8¾in: 222mm) Sunderland pink lustre jug. One side bears a transfer print of the square-rigged ship* Northumberland, *which carried Napoleon to exile on Elba and was a great favourite for jug decoration. The reverse has a Masonic theme containing the words*

The world is in pain
Our secrets to gain
But still let them wonder and gaze on
They ne'er can divine
The word nor the sign
Of a free and an Accepted
MASON

Colour Plate 10. *A moulded Staffordshire jug of a popular design, the decorative treatment varying, with some jugs featuring pink lustre highlights only and some, as here, combining lustre with enamel colours. c.1820s. Ht 4¼in: 114mm.*

Colour Plate 11. *An attractive small plate with a moulded border and pink lustre and green, yellow and chestnut-red enamel decoration. c.1820s. Dia 6¾in: 171mm.*

Colour Plate 12. *An exceptionally finely potted and decorated pottery jug, probably Staffordshire. It combines pink resist lustre on the main part of the body enlivened by touches of enamel colours, with the very skilful freehand use of lustre for the frieze and on the rim and handle. c.1820s. Ht 5½in: 140mm.*

Plate 16. A fine example of a Staffordshire harvest jug with the decorative design carried out with great skill and precision. Pink lustre trim. c.1820-1830.

(Brighton Museum and Art Gallery)

pieces were intended to look as if they were, in fact, solid silver. Teapots, sucriers, cream jugs, salt and pepper pots and many other things were cast or moulded in pottery, complete with the traditional fluting, to resemble, for those who could not afford the real thing, the silver tea services of the well-to-do. Dipped in silver lustre, the best of these looked quite realistic, though there were also many very crude examples that one cannot imagine fooling anybody except at a distance. The year 1840, and with it the introduction of the comparatively cheap electroplating, which replaced the traditional Sheffield plate, brought an end to this rather harmless deception. Candlesticks and figurines were among many other things that received over-all lustring in platinum.

Another form of over-all lustring, practised quite widely by Davenport and others, was to cover a pot with a thin wash of pink lustre which formed the background to a transfer print design, usually in black and often of an oriental character, an example of which is shown in Plate 59. However, probably the most widely used over-all lustring was in copper, carried out by many of the ceramic centres. From them came a vast outpouring of jugs, goblets and other items for the cheapest end of the market. A quick dip and they would be done, with a minimum cost in both labour and materials, though some did have an additional dab or two of enamel applied to brighten them up a little. Most of the lustring was of a reasonable standard but it could be very poor indeed. Whether it was careless preparation of the lustring solution, inadequate firing or for some other reason, a number of the pieces as mentioned earlier, ended up completely lacking the sheen that lustre should have given them.

Nitric Acid; add to these three pints of Common Printers' Tar; stir the whole for one hour in a No. 1 basin, and take particular care to prevent it boiling over; then let it stand for four days; afterwards pour off the top portion and add 1 lb. of Venus Turpentine; stir the whole together for three hours; throw away the remained sediment. The lustre must now be worked in Turpentine if required for use; the older the Lustre is before being used the better it works.

Mrs des Fontaines adds 'This is a metallic lustre but because iron is a base metal it was converted during the firing to a film, not of free metal, but of iron oxide'. She also comments, with some justification, that the preparation must have been very tedious. The use of horse shoe nails for the iron is a nice contemporary touch.

Over-all lustring

This was the most basic form of lustre decoration, in which the whole body of a pot would be covered in a uniform coating of lustre by dipping it in the lustre solution. Sometimes the covering would be both inside and outside the pot, but it was perhaps more usual for the lustre on the inside to be confined to a narrow band round the rim. To achieve this, the pot would be inverted and dipped only to the same depth as the width of the band.

A good example of over-all lustring was the mock Georgian silverware made in considerable quantities in the first half of the nineteenth century, where the individual

'Cottage' or 'Primitive'-style decoration

This has already been touched on in the previous chapter as a form of decoration carried out with bold strokes of the brush and depicting predominantly rural scenes. Almost always it was done in pink lustre on a light ground, though it can look most effective on a deep blue glaze (Colour Plate 15). It was used extensively on Staffordshire wares (both pottery and porcelain), and on those from the north-eastern potteries; also on those from Swansea and neighbouring Llanelli, from Yorkshire and, in fact, from pretty well every factory where any form of lustre was produced, including those north of the border in Scotland. However, there is little, if anything, to distinguish examples of this form of decoration as the work of one centre or another, and what clues there are are rather tenuous. There are, for instance, a number of pieces, including teawares and jugs (Colour Plate 8), that have a very distinctive bird on them, which might indicate that they came from a

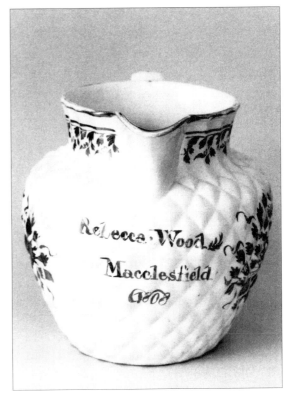

Plates 17 and 18. *Two views of a creamware 'pineapple' jug impressed MEIGH, which should be compared with the Harley jug in Plate 61. This one bears the inscription 'Rebecca Wood, Macclesfield, 1808', while another similar jug with the Meigh mark, illustrated in Gibson and Godden's* Collecting Lustreware, *also has an inscription mentioning the same*

Cheshire town. These are not, apparently, the only ones with this link, and the suggestion has come from Rodney Hampson that there could well have been a Macclesfield decorating establishment which carried out work for Job Meigh and for Harley. (Blakey Collection)

common source. One can, however, never be quite sure because, if a successful line was put on the market by one manufacturer, others would copy it without scruple. This certainly applied with 'cottage-style' decoration, but who was the first in this particular field is anybody's guess.

To go into a little more detail, with very few exceptions the subjects depicted were buildings, cottages of various kinds set amidst groves of trees. However, churches and chapels, large houses, public houses and even castles were all featured, together with a number of buildings showing considerable imagination and fitting into no known category! It was rare for any of these pictures to contain human figures, presumably because the drawing of people would be beyond the ability of the type of decorator (often children) employed on this kind of work. 'Cottage-style' decoration was generally, though by no means always, confined to the cheaper end of the market. Dawson of Sunderland and Sewell in Newcastle were two firms which, however, used it on comparatively sophisticated pieces with unexpectedly happy results.

Lustre was applied with a brush in many other ways, notably on jugs and other pieces from Sunderland and Newcastle, on which the great swirls of pink and sometimes orange (iron) lustre were such a distinguishing feature, though it was imitated to some extent by the Middlesbrough and Stockton potteries further down the north-east coast.

As well as the examples described above, lustre on its own, in all three forms – silver, copper and pink – was used extensively for decorating the rims of jugs and other vessels and for bands of various widths round their circumference.

Resist lustring

Some of the most beautiful and finely-worked lustreware made use of this type of decoration, though surprisingly it does not appear to have been carried out in all the ceramic areas. Certainly it occurred on Staffordshire pieces and there are examples that show that it was practised by the Cambrian Pottery in Wales, and possibly by the Liverpool Herculaneum pottery. There must be a question mark against the names Sunderland and Newcastle, but there is little doubt that the finest of all can be attributed to Leeds. Most resist lustre was carried out in silver, but Leeds and possibly a few others used other types of lustre, notably the most attractive mauve (as opposed to purple), which must have come from a variation in the standard pink lustre recipe.

The resist process, in which the lustre forms the background out of which the design was cut, made use of the principle that, if part of an object has a thin coating of a greasy substance, and the rest is untouched, the greasy part will repel water and the rest will be wetted. In resist lustre the surface to be treated was glazed pottery or porcelain with a size taking the place of grease as a

Colour Plate 13. *Left: a porcelain saucer combining pink lustre banding with a beautifully executed brown bat print of sprays of flowers. The right-hand* *saucer has the more usual 'cottage' style decoration. c.1820-1830. Dia 5½in: 140mm.*

Colour Plate 14. *This lustre jug has, in view of the high standard of the silver resist work, a surprisingly crudely executed Chinese scene in bright enamel colours in the reserves on each side. More familiar are jugs with a robin of a much more acceptable standard in place of the chinoiserie. Probably Staffordshire, c.1830. Ht 4in: 102mm.*

Colour Plate 15. *Very much a Sunderland jug in style and shape, but the pink lustre decoration on the blue slip is not familiar in the north-east. Possibly Sunderland but more likely Staffordshire. c.1820s. Ht 6in: 152mm.*

Colour Plate 16. *The combination of lustre and blue and white underglazed pottery is not common, but that it can be effective is shown by this jug with its coppery pink lustre outlining the building and trees of this eastern (Indian?) scene. Probably Staffordshire, c.1820s. Ht 7in: 178mm.*

Colour Plate 17. *A very striking Staffordshire jug of a familiar form, but unusual in the lightness of touch and sophistication of its coloured transfer-printed decoration. The rim and trim are in silver lustre. c.1820s. Ht 6in: 152mm.*

Plate 19. *A large marriage jug inscribed for Edward and Elizabeth Massey, 1824. The banding on the neck is copper lustre and the spout is pink. It is difficult to say just what the main central design represents as it is made up of so many elements with no obvious link. They include a scales, a bluebird, crossed keys, the sun, an hour glass, a pair of dividers and set-square and various other items difficult to identify, the whole surmounted by a banner proclaiming 'Protestant Ascendency, Holiness to the Lord'. The figure underneath holding a cross is Faith. Probably Staffordshire.* (Tolson Collection)

pink lustred items and both the alternative names describe its appearance very well. An over-all coating of pink lustre would be sprayed with fine drops of oil while still wet. These formed small pools on the surface which, when fired and the oil had burned away, left the surface mottled. The amount of mottling, which was used extensively by the potteries of the north-east and most of the others probably to a lesser extent, could be varied considerably, depending on the amount of oil used.

Variegated lustre

Used principally by Wedgwood and by Spode, this used to be known, for no very obvious reason, as 'Moonlight lustre'. However, the term has fallen out of favour and variegated lustre is now considered correct. Basically, it is pink lustre which, according to contemporary record, was 'mixed with sweet wort and laid on with a feather', which gives a unique finish quite different from that obtained with a brush (pencil). Sometimes additions to the lustre broaden the range of tones, tiny streaks of orange, derived from iron in the mixture, frequently appearing. Fine examples of variegated lustre are the components of the very popular Wedgwood dessert service, in which the items were modelled on scallop, nautilus and other shells. The Spode version of variegated lustre was achieved with a brush rather than a feather, there were no additional colours and the over-all effect was more uniform.

Transfer printing

The use of transfer prints to decorate pottery and porcelain was not, of course, confined to lustreware, though lustred items made great use of them. Sometimes they were the major element in the decoration with maybe just a little bit of lustre trim. At other times, especially on Sunderland and Newcastle wares, they were so much a part of the whole decorative scheme that they really cannot be regarded as separate entities. The prints without the lustre or the lustre without the prints would count for nothing, so cleverly were they combined. The prints were created as follows:

The design, a picture or perhaps lettering, would first be engraved on a copper plate. Special warmed printing ink would be applied to this and, when the plate was wiped, the ink would be retained only in the engraved lines. The copper plate was then pressed evenly on to a special, extra-strong, tissue paper which picked up the ink from the lines so that the design was transferred from one to the other. The tissue paper was then applied to the glazed pottery or porcelain, transferring the design once more. When the pot was immersed in cold water this had the effect of hardening the ink, leaving the transferred design on its

repellent. This size was often a mixture of sugar and glycerine, which made sure that the lustre did not adhere where it was not wanted.

The design was first outlined very faintly in pencil on the glazed pot and and then, using a fine brush, filled in with a coating of size. When this had dried the pot would be dipped into the lustring solution to just below the rim if the interior was to be left unlustred. The whole thing would then be inverted and the rim itself dipped separately. The lustre would now have adhered to the unsized parts of the pot and, after drying once more, the size was washed away with water. Firing came next and for the first time it would really be possible to see the beauty of the design. As already mentioned, the lustre would form the background, outlining the design which would be in the colour of the clay in which the pot was made or that of a slip applied to it before the lustring. Some of the most striking resist work was done on pots covered with a canary-yellow slip or glaze. Silver lustre looks particularly well in this combination and was used often enough for the generic term Canary Lustre to be coined. This embraced not just resist work but silver lustre rims, banding and other decoration painted on the yellow ground.

Splashed or mottled lustre

This form of decoration was confined almost entirely to

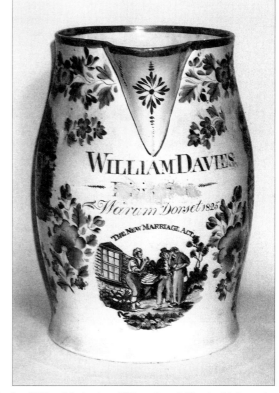

Plates 20 and 21. *Two views of a beautifully decorated jug, part of the inscription indicating that it was made in celebration of The New Marriage Act of 1823. This covered the chief points of the law relative to marriage in Great Britain. It may also be the marriage jug of William Davies whose name appears on it, together* *with the date 1825 and the location of 'Warum Dorset'. There is pink lustre trim and enamel-coloured transfer prints. Probably Staffordshire.*

(Brighton Museum and Art Gallery)

surface as the sodden paper floated away.

This process was comparatively easy to carry out on a flat or almost flat surface, but more skill was needed when applying the tissue paper to the side of a jug of typical Sunderland shape, where the surface was not only curved, but curved in two directions not unlike, in fact, the surface of a globe. Occasionally one can spot where a print has been creased by over-hasty application, but generally speaking the standard was reasonably high. The other fault sometimes found − if, indeed, it is a fault rather than a charming eccentricity − is when the transfer has been applied to something of a size or shape for which it was not designed. It is usually obvious when this has happened and the reason for it was, of course, economy. The Sunderland butter pot in Colour Plate 108 is an example of a print applied to an item smaller than that for which it was originally intended.

The more pieces of pottery on which a print from a single (and expensive) copper plate could be used the better, and for the cheaper end of the market it did not matter too much if they looked a little odd. But even for the more expensive pieces, it can be seen that transfer printing was a comparatively quick and easy way of decorating a series of identical items in a uniform way. Having mentioned Sunderland as a major user of transfer print decoration, samples from there can be used to give our first examples of how lustre and the prints were combined to maximum effect.

A recurring theme on the big, bulbous Sunderland jugs

and, indeed, on many of their other pieces, was a series of pictures of the iron bridge over the river Wear on which Sunderland is situated. Almost as common were mock heraldic designs of The Farmers' Arms or The Blacksmiths' Arms, designs celebrating organisations such as the Oddfellows and the Masons and, not surprisingly as Sunderland was an important ship building centre, any number of pictures of ships in full sail. The reverse side of these jugs and any blank space left on other items would be taken up with a doggerel rhyme, often fully illustrated and surrounded by wreaths of flowers or any other suitable (or sometimes unsuitable) decoration. Pottery wall plaques from Sunderland would carry prints of short religious texts or profound, if platitudinous, sayings. A number featured portraits of religious leaders such as John Wesley, or contemporary politicians.

Apart from Ball Brothers, who also used purple and brown, the Sunderland prints were generally black, but they would be embellished with enamel colours. Almost always pink lustre was added, often in the form of borders, to give them that extra sparkle. These would be backed by the usual pink lustre swirls or sometimes mottled lustre or a combination of the two. Wall plaques would have many of the print designs from other items in the centre and would be framed in lustre, sometimes pink but often copper or a combination of both. Some would also have mottled lustre decoration.

Nearby Newcastle upon Tyne combined transfer prints

Colour Plate 18. *A particularly good example of a moulded octagonal jug, a type popular in many ceramic centres, c.1840 onwards. There is pink lustre round the rim and base and two different enamel-coloured transfer prints of floral sprays appear in alternate lustre-framed panels. Ht 7in: 178mm.*

Colour Plate 19. *A Staffordshire jug of very popular and pleasing design which is found with many different decorative schemes and with minor differences in the mouldings (Colour Plate 84). This one has pink lustre banding and trim and two particularly fine bat prints of stag hunting, a different one on each side. c.1830. Ht 6in: 152mm.*

Colour Plate 20. *A pink lustre trimmed porcelain cup and saucer, the transfer printed in puce before hand colouring with enamels. The print is yet another version of that shown in Plate 23. Staffordshire, c.1820s. Saucer dia 5½in: 140mm.*

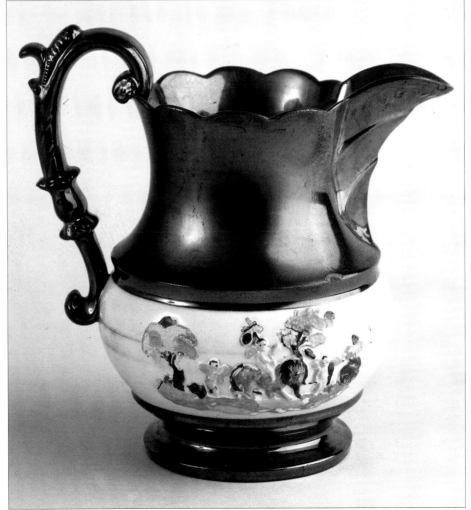

Colour Plate 21. *A very typical copper lustre jug of the 1820-1830 period, made in their thousands for the mass market by a number of centres. The coloured enamel of the sprigging shows up well on the white slip banding. Ht 6½in: 165mm.*

Plate 22. *Two portrait busts. Left: John Wesley, decorated in silver lustre on a buff body, 10½in: 267mm high. Right: William Shakespeare, 8½in: 216mm high. Here only the base is splashed pink lustre, the rest of the decoration being in enamel colours. Staffordshire, c.1830.* (Gutman Collection)

and lustre in much the same way, even using many of the same subjects, including on occasion Sunderland's own Wear Bridge. Potteries elsewhere had a different approach, the transfers frequently being based on book illustrations of rural scenes, stately homes and castles or else derived from the political and other topical prints which were such a feature of the period. A number of potteries in both Newcastle and Sunderland used printing plates supplied to them by the Beilby/Bewick workshops. Miss A.V. Gill's *The Potteries of the Tyne and Wear, and Their Dealings with the Beilby/Bewick Workshop* (an offprint from *Archaelogia Aeliana,* published by The Society of Antiquaries, Newcastle upon Tyne), tells us that the workshop was set up for 'the engraving and repairing of plates (copper) and wood'. Thomas Bewick was, of course, a noted wood engraver and book illustrator. Some twenty potteries were their customers, both in Newcastle and Sunderland. Account books detail transactions including those with the North Hylton Pottery, Sunderland, specifying engravings of the Sunderland Bridge, 'Vicar and Moses', 'Nankia', 'the Miller, his Son and their Ass', and 'Poor Jack'. The 'Garrison' Pottery used their engravings of 'The Tythe Pig', 'Air Balloon', and again Sunderland Bridge and 'Poor Jack'. The latter was obviously popular as Scott's Southwick Pottery used him as well, together with the inevitable bridge and the flower borders that were exclusive to Scott. Sewell of Newcastle was also a frequent user of Beilby/Bewick engravings. The prints from them would usually be contained in a reserve deliberately left on a jug which was otherwise lustred over-all. The combinations were endless as the illustrations in this book will show.

Bat printing

This way of producing coloured prints without the use of

added enamel colours had been first launched in the last part of the eighteenth century, in 1760 to be precise, though it was not until a year or two after the introduction of lustreware that it was sufficiently developed to make it a commercial proposition. An engraved copper plate was employed, just as with a transfer print, though a special oil rather than printing ink was used. The surface of the plate wiped, this was retained in the etched lines and from these transferred to the bat, which was a gelatinous sheet. The flexibility of this enabled it to be applied to a curved glazed surface and the oil lines were once more transferred, this time to the glaze. Following a pre-determined pattern so that they would end up in places appropriate to the engraved picture, different coloured powdered pigments would be dusted on to the oil lines, a process requiring considerable skill, but producing in the end a most effective result when the pot was fired. The oil vaporised and the coloured pigments fused with the glaze. Bat printing could, of course, be carried out using one colour only, though this was not taking full advantage of its possibilities. It was often employed in combination with lustre in the way that transfer printing was, but was a more complex process and so not carried out for the cheapest end of the market. It was more usual for bat prints to be monochrome.

Decoration with enamels

In writing earlier about copper lustred items the impression may have been given that all of it was rather dull and dowdy. This was, however, far from the case, for it was used at its best in conjunction with many other kinds of decoration. The embellishing of transfer prints with enamel colours has already been mentioned. Such prints might occur in reserves on copper lustre, but enamels were used on this type of lustre in a number of other ways. However, before going on to describe how this was done, it might be as well to say a little more about copper lustre itself.

Very few pieces of lustreware of any sort bear makers' marks and this applies perhaps more to copper lustre than any other. It was enormously popular in its day and made, as has been said, in vast quantities, but placing items in any one of the main ceramic producing areas is next to impossible. There is little doubt that it was produced everywhere, from Swansea to Glasgow and all stops in between, but what came from where is mostly anybody's guess. The shapes or handles, moulding or decoration on a few copper individual lustre pieces make it at least likely that they came from a particular factory, and in some cases they can be matched with wasters found in excavations of a known site. This has happened with a number of Enoch Wood wares, but it is the exception to the rule.

The point is well made by E. Morton Nance in his massive and definitive *The Pottery and Porcelain of Swansea and Nantgarw.* In this he says: 'Similarity of paste and glaze and the identity of shapes and decoration with ordinary earthenware known to have been manufactured in Swansea may often lead one to a correct conclusion, but even then one cannot be absolutely certain, for the paste and glaze of Swansea earthenware, as well as its shapes, are very like, if not identical with, various Staffordshire and Yorkshire products'. To this he could well have added all the other ceramic producing areas. In all of them there are today antiques shops in which the copper lustreware they display is claimed, with apparent confidence, to be of local manufacture. This may well be true in a few instances, especially for pieces known to have been in the possession of a local family since the days when the neighbourhood pot works was in full production, but in most cases it will be wishful thinking to make the pot more interesting to a prospective buyer.

However, all this is something of a diversion from the subject of decorating with enamels. There were some fine copper lustre pieces produced, notably by the firms of Wood and Caldwell and Enoch Wood, which often combined copper lustre with a wide banding of a notably mellow blue glaze, to which gaily coloured enamel sprigging was added. A number of these bear the maker's mark, so we do know where they came from. In other cases the banding might be mottled pink lustre so that there was a combination of both pink and copper on the same jug. Brightly enamelled sprigging was often used on both pink and copper lustre, favourite subjects being wreaths of flowers and other floral devices and putti, as often as not disporting themselves with goats harnessed to chariots. This mythical theme was also carried out in white sprigging, together with other white trim, on a series of very distinctive copper lustre jugs attributed by Baker and John to the Shorthose factory, being linked by a similarity to a marked cup and saucer.

The extensive use of lustre, silver, pink and copper, for borders, for reserves, for banding and for the highlighting

Plate 23. *A very small (4in: 102mm dia) wall plaque and a large (5¼in: 146mm dia) child's plate with, apparently, the same transfer print in deep pink on both. Close examination, however, shows differences in the engravings, and yet other close copies are known on cups and saucers. The rims of both are in dark pink lustre. Staffordshire, c.1825.*

of rims has already been touched on.

Here is a contemporary recipe for making enamel:

PROCESS 78
To make Enamel Blue
Take 16 Parts of Flint Glass
    5   of Red Lead
    2   of Nitre of Potash
    2½ of Blue Calx
For these blue enamels the materials must be calcined in an air furnace or glazing oven, and caution should be observed that they are not too finely ground at the mill, in order to prevent it from crazing or chipping after being burnt on the pieces of ware, which this colour is very susceptible of doing.

Stencilled lustre
The process, very rarely used as it was difficult to achieve

Plate 24. *Three typical silver lustre jugs of the 1812-1815 period. The centre one could be from the Leeds pottery and the other two, which combine enamel colours with the lustre, are likely to be Staffordshire. The left-hand jug shows the bust of Sir Francis Burdett in a canary-yellow coat. He was the son-in-law of the founder of Coutts bank and a great parliamentarian, whose political activities ended with his being committed to the Tower of London! He was, however, generally very popular, and engravings of his likeness frequently feature on Staffordshire wares.* (Russell, Baldwin & Bright)

Colour Plates 22 and 23. *Two very fine moulded pink lustre jugs, both with 'cottage' style decoration in the reserves, but with a great deal of more sophisticated decoration surrounding it, carried out both in lustre and green enamel. The first* *jug, oval in section and 6½in: 152mm high, is probably Staffordshire, c.1820. The jug with the caryatid handle, is thought to be from Thomas Fell's St Peter's Pottery in Newcastle, c.1820-1830. Ht 6½in: 165mm.*

Colour Plate 24. *An 8in: 203mm diameter yellow-glaze plate decorated with silver lustre and with the verticulated border in red and green enamel. Beside it is a yellow-glaze mug with a silver lustre rim and an elaborate, scrolled transfer print design on the side incorporating the words (capitalisation* *as shown) 'SUPER FINE PORTER' with, underneath this, 'PEACE and Roast BEEF to the Friends of LIBERTY'. Both probably Staffordshire c.1820.* *(Gutman Collection)*

Colour Plate 25. *A 3½in 89mm high mug and a 5in: 127mm high jug, attractively decorated in silver lustre over a blue ground. Probably Staffordshire, c.1830.* (Gutman Collection)

good results, produced the reverse of resist work. The design itself would be in lustre and the background the natural colour of the pot or glaze with which it had been treated. The firm of John Davenport was credited with its introduction early in the nineteenth century.

The stencil, from a drawn design, would be cut from paper, which would be dampened and then spread over the surface of the pot, after which the whole thing would be given a coating of glue size. When this was dry, the paper pattern was peeled off, leaving the parts of the pot which it had not covered still with their coating of size. When the pot was dipped in a lustre solution it adhered to the unsized areas and the pattern was revealed as soon as the pot was fired.

Fairyland lustre

This decoration, exclusive to the Wedgwood factory, was a twentieth century development created by Daisy Makeig-Jones, who joined Wedgwood as a trainee decorator in 1909. She was a quick learner and soon achieved a sound know-ledge of the various decorating techniques. Eventually she was allowed to branch out on her own, making full use of the commercial lustre preparations by then available in a wide range of colours. These she used in many ways and combinations, sometimes applying them over a background of under-glaze staining or mottling, and with them created fantastic designs often based on fairyland scenes. Much of her design work was completely original, but she did at times draw inspiration from leading fairytale book illustrators of the day like Edmund Dulac, H.J. Ford and Kay Nielsen. She became a force to be reckoned with in the Wedgwood organisation and, in due course, a supervisor of other decorators who carried out work under her direction,

so that all Fairyland Lustre was not actually by her hand. There are, however, a number of pieces that bear her incised monogram, though these should not be confused with some with the monogram created from an engraved plate.

Miss Makeig-Jones left Wedgwood early in 1931, when production of her lustre ceased. Her process had always been comparatively expensive to carry out, which led to a relatively limited output and means that Fairyland Lustre is much sought after by collectors today.

Colour Plate 26. *A Sunderland wall plaque with one of the customary religious admonitions, but with an exceptionally wide pink lustre border into which floral sprays are moulded. c.1820s. 8¼in: 210mm x 8in: 203mm.*

CHAPTER III

Collecting Lustreware

Collecting lustreware is, of course, what this book is all about, and the descriptions of the wares given in later chapters should be useful for attributing and possibly dating pieces collected by the enthusiast, though not all by any means are of certain origin. However, the design or decoration of an unmarked lustred pot may, in isolation, make it a mystery, but matching it with another similar piece (not necessarily also lustred) from a known factory, makes identification of source fairly certain.

It has been possible to make a positive identification of quite a few pieces of lustreware illustrated in this book because they bear the makers' marks. It is primarily because they are marked that they have been chosen, so the products of particular potteries can be shown and commented on with a degree of certainty. However, it cannot be stressed too strongly that these pieces are the exception and a lustre collector will be exceedingly fortunate if he finds any marks at all. The reasons for this are as follows.

During the eighteenth and early nineteenth centuries the provincial potteries tended to do their selling to the public through retailers who preferred to keep their customers in ignorance of their sources of supply (so that it would not be possible for the customer to bypass the retailer in future deals and do business direct with the manufacturer). No marking was therefore part of the original contracts negotiated with most potteries, though

there were exceptions. Companies like that of Josiah Spode and Davenport carried sufficient prestige to enable them to set their own terms and they marked their wares accordingly. The other exception was for goods sold abroad, where a maker's mark would be welcomed as a guarantee of authenticity. It was probably because so much of the work they produced went into the export market that the pottery of Sunderland and Newcastle was often impressed with the names of the manufacturers.

Although a collector will be extremely lucky if he finds a piece of lustreware that is marked, such pieces do exist and may turn up from time to time. When found, they add greatly to the excitement of the chase, so it will be useful to know something about the forms they will take.

First there are incised marks in which the name of the pottery, or perhaps the initials of its owner, are scratched into the soft clay of the body before firing or decoration. This will have been done by hand and thus will lack the precision and neatness of an impressed mark which is made with a metal die at the same stage of manufacture. As the clay for the pieces to be marked will not have been hardened by firing, the pressure needed to apply the die could cause damage, particularly on something like a hollow pot. Thus, unless the piece was very sturdy, the mark would be placed close to the rim, an extra sharp die might be used, or the mark might be so tiny that little pressure was needed. Some manufacturers elected not to use

Plate 25. *This cup and saucer from a tea service, in a style extremely popular in its day, is decorated with what can only be described as a garishly-coloured transfer print. It is predominantly in bright reds and yellows, and the pair have* pink lustre rims and internal banding, which hardly adds harmony to the overall colour scheme. c.1825 and probably Staffordshire.

Plate 26. *The handle of this jug is most distinctive, but so far has not helped in placing it with a manufacturer. Probably Staffordshire, however, and copper lustre with a white slip inside and out. The depiction of 'Charity' in a purple transfer print on both sides of the jug is framed in a lustre cartouche. c.1820. Ht 6in: 152mm. (See Griselda Lewis'* Collectors' History of English Pottery *for 'Faith' and 'Hope'.)* (Blakey Collection)

impressed marks at all.

Printed marks come next, and could be applied over the glaze with a rubber stamp. However, in the nineteenth century, transfer prints from copper plates were more generally used. Often a printed mark would be surrounded by a decorative cartouche, and sometimes it carried the pattern name of the piece on which it appeared rather than the maker's name. On pottery from the north-east – Sunderland and Newcastle – the maker's name was

Plate 27. *A creamware mug with pink lustre banding, matching the jug shown in Plate 35b in John and Baker's* Old English Lustre Pottery. *Probably Staffordshire, c.1830. Ht 3¾in: 95mm.* (Blakey Collection)

sometimes incorporated into the main transfer print on the sides of a mug or jug rather than appearing on the base.

Painted marks were applied by hand over the glaze during or after decoration. Sometimes individual decorators' marks would be included.

When teawares bear an impressed mark, this is usually on the saucer or plate and very rarely on the cup. On a teapot it would appear near an edge. The reasons for this were that flatwares would be supported during manufacture on the side opposite to where the name was impressed. At the same time, it was almost impossible to support the sides of hollow pieces like jugs, cups or teapots. It might be added that, even when a piece of lustreware has been impressed with a maker's name, it is not always easy to read. The die may have been carelessly applied or the impressed letters be at least partially obscured by a slip or a glaze.

Before leaving the subject of marks, a further point might be made. For one reason or another – perhaps a change in partnership – a great number of the potteries altered the form of their marks from time to time. Thus one firm would end up with a number of different ones, though it might simply involve, in each case, a revised style of lettering and no change in the wording. Thus, if the years are known when this revision occurred, the design of a mark may help to date a particular ware. Wedgwood, which because of its longevity as a company probably had more different marks than most, have an information sheet detailing them all, which enables their products to be dated with considerable precision.

What is it about lustre-decorated pottery and porcelain that gives it its special attraction? It cannot just be only the

Colour Plate 27. *A porcelain pink lustre-decorated plate, Staffordshire, c.1820-1830. Dia 8½in: 216mm.*

Colour Plate 28. *Dishes like this gave great scope for attractive decoration like that shown here, with its striking leaf pattern in pink lustre. Probably Staffordshire, c.1820s. Dia 8in: 203mm.*

Colour Plate 29. *A Staffordshire cup and saucer, the central motif freely painted without the backing of a transfer print to define it, so that there are small variations between the cup and saucer and the other pieces of the tea set from which it comes. The decorative leaf border on the saucer and the inside rim of the cup are in pink lustre. c.1820s. Saucer dia 5½in: 140mm*

Colour Plate 30. *A Staffordshire porcelain cup and saucer with pink lustre decoration of very high quality. The small flowers in the pattern are in chestnut-red enamel. c.1825. Saucer dia 5½in: 140mm.*

Colour Plate 31. *Compare the pink lustre and enamel colour treatment of this jug with that of the other, yellow-glazed version in Colour Plates 41 and 42.*

Plate 28. *A large (5¾in: 146mm) mask jug decorated with a topical political theme, dating from the 1840s. The coloured transfer print shows, on one side, Jack Frost attacking BONY in Russia, who is thanking his stars that he got out of the hands of 'them Damn Cossacks'. On the other, the one shown here, is 'Little BONY sneaking into Paris with a white feather in his tail'. The mask, neck and unusual swan handle are silver lustre.*
(Gutman Collection)

appeal of unsophisticated folk-art, a category into which much lustreware might be placed, for lustre is also used on fine porcelain from factories such as Miles Mason, New Hall and Spode. As we know, it was first used as a novelty to add sparkle to ceramic decoration and, in realising that aim, achieved a popularity that few could have forecast. That must still help to make up its appeal, but I think that a large part of the excitement in lustre collecting is coming on the unexpected. There is something for everyone, from the crude humour immortalised in the decoration of chamber pots from Sunderland, to the extremely fine silver resist lustre work carried out by the Leeds decorators, or to the Sewell vase from Newcastle shown in Colour Plate 130. The variety is seemingly infinite and, just as one arrives at the point of apparently having a pretty representative collection, some quite new and almost always fascinating lustred object is discovered sitting on a dealer's stand, with a smug certainty of being bought by someone else if you do not grab it quickly.

The reason for this variety has already been touched on. Many of the potteries in the northern half of the United Kingdom in the nineteenth century did at one time or another experiment with lustre decoration. With some of them experimentation was as far as it went, but in many cases even these trials must have produced wares which were tried out in the market. Though the production run might have been limited to no more than a hundred or so and lustre then abandoned for one reason or another, a number of the items from that hundred could have survived to today.

However, even if one sets aside these really exceptional

pieces, the number of Staffordshire potteries turning out lustre-decorated wares went well into three figures (though not necessarily all at the same time), to which must be added those of the north-east, Scotland, South Wales, Yorkshire, possibly Liverpool, and a number outside the main centres. Is it any wonder that the variety is so vast, not

Plate 29. *A grotesquely ugly but nevertheless very popular type of mask jug with silver lustre trim, probably from Harley of Lane End, c.1815. The masks and flower decorations are in chestnut red. (See also Colour Plate 91.)*
(Gutman Collection)

only in the design of the pots but in the styles of decoration?

Lustre decoration was carried out on many kinds of ceramic material, from fine porcelain to quite unrefined earthenware, taking in creamware, pearlware, ironstone and all the rest. As scarcely any of it was marked, the lustre collector should, ideally, have an encyclopedic knowledge of all the distinguishing characteristics of the wares from every single one of the many companies producing it. Few, if any, people come into this category, however, and a new collector need not despair. One can get along very happily with a reasonable knowledge of the wares from comparatively few factories and your collecting can be, if you choose, confined to the products of only one area. But it is amazing how quickly one's breadth of knowledge does build up, in which regular visits to museums and other collections must play a part, together with wide reading, exchange of information with people with the same interests, such as ceramic dealers or by joining an antiques society.

If one decides to concentrate in the beginning on a single area of lustre collecting, there is probably no better place to choose than the potteries of the north-east coast of England. This is because the number of companies involved with lustre decoration was comparatively small and because they did, collectively, develop a very definite style that was all their own. Their total output was large and a great deal of it has survived, so there is certainly enough to encourage a beginner to keep going, and it is varied enough to keep him or her eagerly on the lookout for more.

The areas concerned are, of course, Sunderland and Newcastle. One is particularly well off with Sunderland as its ceramic industry has been well researched by the enthusiastic staff of the Tyne and Wear museums and the results detailed in *Sunderland Pottery* by John C. Baker. Comprehensive as this is, however, it has not at the time of writing been reprinted since the fifth edition in 1984 and in a few minor areas is now not quite up to date. For instance, it reproduces pictures of some forty or so different engravings of the Sunderland Iron Bridge that have been used as transfer print decorations on Sunderland jugs, bowls and so on, but unknown engraved versions of the bridge are still occasionally being found. Discovering one would be a considerable scoop for any collector. So, too, would be the discovery of a new rhyme on one of the Sunderland pieces. All rhymes known at the time of its publication are recorded in *Sunderland Pottery,* together with the names of the particular pottery or potteries that used them. This, coupled with the fact that quite a

Plates 30 and 31. *A pair of pink lustre teapots, c.1820, with contrasting decorative schemes, both robustly potted and very much for everyday use. That with the 'cottage' style decoration is possibly from Sunderland and the other one, with the more sophisticated transfer print, is of unknown origin.*

reasonable proportion of the wares was marked and that Sunderland Museum and Art Gallery has on display a very representative collection grouped company by company, means that the tiro collector is really rather well off for information. At the same time, there are enough areas of uncertainty left and enough facts still to be unearthed to keep interest very much alive. A warning is needed, however, about possible pitfalls.

A good deal of Sunderland ware has been and is still being reproduced. This will be covered when we deal with lustre reproductions in general, but there is a second misleading factor liable to crop up which has already been touched on. The name 'Sunderland' has become, to much of the antiques trade, a generic term for pink lustre. Anything with pink lustre on it, be it from Staffordshire, Swansea or one of the Yorkshire potteries, seems automatically to be labelled as Sunderland, even though it may be a porcelain cup and saucer. Porcelain was never

Colour Plate 32. *A pair of moulded jugs, one seven-sided and one with ten facets, very attractively decorated with coloured transfer prints and a pink lustre trim. This type of jug was produced in large quantities in Staffordshire and was enormously popular. c.1840. Hts (right) 7in: 178mm and (left) 6½in: 165mm.*

Colour Plate 33. *An oval section jug decorated in pink lustre and enamel colours, the moulded frieze round the body showing a particular hunting scene, versions of which can be found again and again on Staffordshire wares of all kinds. The lightness of the jug suggests an early date, say 1815. Ht 4¼in:108mm.*

Colour Plate 34. *Two mugs combining broad copper lustre banding with the ever-popular chinoiserie designs. c.1820. Hts 3¼in: 83mm and 2in: 51mm.*

Colour Plate 35. *Two moulded pink lustre jugs decorated with virtually the same stag-hunting scene and one with the same unusual caryatid handle as the jug in Colour Plate 23, suggesting that all three came from the same pottery – possibly Thomas Fell of Newcastle. c.1820s. Ht 4½in:114mm.*

NORTHUMBERLAND
Life Boat.

WHEREAS the BOAT HOUSE DOOR, has of late been repeatedly broken open, and the Boat taken away, without the sanction of the Committee, at same time leaving the House open, and thereby exposing the Boat's Stores to pilferage, in order to put a stop to such Outrageous proceedings, the Committee are determined to punish any Person or Persons found guilty of such Conduct in future.

The Committee also determine, that the Crew who may go off with the Boat, shall on their return moor the Boat, and at a proper Time of the Tide, assist in getting her into the House, and in order to have the Expence of the Boat going off amicably settled, Persons liable to pay, are requested not to settle with any Person, without a written Order for the same, signed by two of the acting Committee.

A **KEY** of the BOAT HOUSE DOOR is lodged with the TIDE SURVEYORS, at the CUSTOM HOUSE WATCH HOUSE, and the Boat will be in constant readiness, to go off in all cases of Danger, to save the Lives of Shipwrecked Mariners, and for no other Purpose whatever.

SHIP-OWNERS are respectfully reminded, that any Ship which has not contributed TEN SHILLINGS AND SIXPENCE to the Fund of the Life Boat, since such Ship became their Property, are liable to pay the whole Expence of the Boat going off (about EIGHT POUNDS) should such Assistance be necessary.

Donations and Subscriptions

will be received by Mr JAMES BURNE, Treasurer ; also by the acting COMMITTEE at NORTH SHIELDS ; or at the CUSTOM-HOUSE, NEWCASTLE.

JOHN HUTCHINSON
WILLIAM REAY
MILES HANN
ROBERT YOUNG } ACTING COMMITTEE.

North Shields, March 12, 1823.

APPLEBY, PRINTER.

Plate 32. *A poster, asking for help to stop vandalism of the North Shields lifeboat and boathouse, headed by a Bewick engraving of the lifeboat in action. A close copy of this is featured in the transfer print on the Newcastle jug in Colour Plate 124. (Tyne and Wear Museums)*

meant wares produced to celebrate historical events and not those one-off presentation pieces that may have been inscribed with the date of a wedding, retirement or other purely domestic occurrence. In passing, one should not assume that a date inscribed on the latter shows the year in which it was made. It could have been chosen from an existing factory pattern and the name and date added later, or perhaps the date represents the birth of the owner rather than the date of presentation. The historical commemorative piece is more likely to be of interest for it will have been manufactured or decorated specially for the occasion, though designs that proved to be very popular might continue to be manufactured for some years after the event. Nevertheless, they can be dated reasonably precisely, which adds materially to their importance but also, unfortunately, to the price. Commemorative wares will cost a great deal more than comparable pieces for which the date can only be estimated.

Many of the Newcastle products and styles of decoration are very close to those of Sunderland, so it is mainly a question for the collector of being able to distinguish one from another. Chapter 5 shows ways in which this can be done, and useful information will be found in R.C. Bell's *Tyneside Pottery*, and in *Maling, the Trademark of Excellence,* by Steven Moore and Catherine Ross.

Ceramic books are, of course, of great help to the collector, but the Staffordshire area was so large and there were so many potteries that no one book could be expected to cover them all in any great detail, though volumes like Dr Geoffrey Godden's *Encyclopaedia of British Porcelain Manufacturers* goes over a great deal of the ground, concentrating, however, as the title implies, on porcelain only. In addition, there are many books dealing with particular factories and some other general histories that usually tend to concentrate on the biggest and most important Staffordshire manufacturers.

A valiant and largely successful attempt to achieve the impossible and cover, in great detail, the whole of the South Wales area was made by E. Morton Nance with his monumental *The Pottery and Porcelain of Swansea and Nantgarw,* though even in this the closely related Llanelly pottery is not covered. A reasonably comprehensive list of books useful to collectors will be found in the bibliography.

The following statement may send a shiver down the

produced at any of the Wearside factories

One could, of course, decide to specialise not just in Sunderland ware, but in Sunderland jugs or plaques, or any other linked range of products. How this can be carried to what might be called enthusiastic excess can be seen in the Hanley Museum at Stoke-on-Trent, where there is a vast collection of cow creamers left to the museum on condition that a considerable number of them must be on constant display. Frog mugs might be another area for specialising, though those from most of the Sunderland potteries are difficult to tell one from another, except by examining the moulding of the frogs, as described in Chapter 5.

Another collecting theme that many people follow up is the seeking out of commemorative lustreware. By this is

Plate 33. *Pink lustreware at its simplest. Two contrasting milk jug shapes decorated in the 'cottage' style, the shorter jug having, in addition, an orange band round the reserve.*

backs of museum curators, but it would be of enormous advantage to collectors if they could handle the exhibits of pottery and porcelain displayed in the cases. Sometimes this will be possible if the collector is able to show that he has a serious purpose for his request and applies to make the necessary arrangements beforehand. Much can be learned just by being able to hold a piece of pottery in the hand and, as one gains experience, just the feel of it may tell you a great deal. Its weight may indicate whether it is an early or late piece (in general the earlier the lighter) and if you can inspect it closely for factory marks or pattern numbers and discover whether it is basic earthenware, more refined creamware, pearlware, ironstone or porcelain, the picture will begin to round out. Clearly museums cannot allow all and sundry to hold and examine their exhibits, but through membership of a ceramic society you are likely to be able to take part in organised visits which will include privileged close inspection of the contents of the show cases.

Handling and close inspection is, of course, essential if you are buying lustreware for your collection. Most reputable dealers will tell you if a piece has hairline cracks or has been restored, but it is much more satisfactory if you can see for yourself just what the extent of the crack or restoration may be. Antiques fairs are a happy hunting ground for collectors but, though items may be datelined and have been 'authenticated' at the better fairs, a thorough knowledge of lustreware is not common and errors in attribution can and do occur. There is, however, more than enough genuine lustreware to be seen at the

more popular general antiques fairs nowadays to encourage those beginners in the field of collecting to look for more. It will not always be of particularly high quality and perhaps largely made up of moulded copper lustre jugs and goblets, plus pink lustre cups and saucers of a run of the mill kind. However, these should not be despised and are the kind of thing that most collectors start with. There is

Plate 34. *A Sunderland bridge mug with the name of the pottery under the engraving blacked out. This would seem to indicate the use of its copper printing plate by a factory other than that which originated it. William Ball bought up the plates when Scott's Southwick Pottery went out of business in 1896, and the use of a floral decoration inside the rim of this mug does suggest that this one came from Scott originally. On the other hand, the mug certainly looks as if it came from a period a good deal earlier than the end of the 19th century and, as there appears to be some damage to the printing plate, perhaps Scott's discarded it as below their standard while they were still in business, not intending that it should be used again.*

(Blakey collection)

Colour Plate 36. *A sucrier decorated with 'cottage'-style pink lustre of a shape popular both in the north-east and in Staffordshire. This one must be from the latter as it is in bone china, and has small, moulded rams' heads on each side, a decorative feature not usually found on the Sunderland versions. c.1820s. Ht 5¼in: 133mm.*

Colour Plate 37. *A small copper lustre teapot typical of hundreds produced in Staffordshire in the 1800s, though the vivid blue slip used for the banding does make it stand out. Ht 5½in: 140mm.*

Colour Plate 38 *A pair of pink lustre Staffordshire jugs of a type that became immensely popular. They had a variety of motifs moulded into the body, and the decorative schemes, by no means all incorporating lustre, also varied widely. The rather strange, four-cornered shape, and the ribbing, might* indicate that the original was based on a metal jug design. The only known example with an impressed maker's mark came from George Weston of Lane End, c.1810-1820, but many were made by others after that date. Hts 5in: 127mm.

Colour Plate 39. *Two bone china pink lustre cream jugs of contrasting styles. The jug decorated with the bat print of crossed shotguns and powder horns and* *a stag's head is likely, from the shape of the handle, to be from the Adams factory, c.1825-1830. Lengths 5in: 127mm, and 5¼in 133mm.*

Colour Plate 40. *Two moulded jugs of a type common quite late in the 19th century, c.1850-1860. The left-hand jug is known as 'The Volunteer' and, apart from featuring the volunteer himself in a rather unlikely pink uniform,* *has a handle moulded in the shape of a musket. The other jug has a colourfully costumed gallery of an outlaw band moulded round the sides. Hts 7½in: 191mm and 6½in: 165mm.*

Plates 35a and 35b. (a) A Sunderland pink lustre frog mug from Dixon Phillips with, in addition to the moulded frog, traditional style decoration incorporating transfer prints, pictures and verses. (b) Two very similar frog mugs from Moore and Co.'s Wear Pottery, but it can be seen that the frogs from the two firms are clearly distinguishable. The moulding of these can be a guide to the origin of a mug as each firm had its own distinctive pattern.
(The Potteries Museum, Hanley, Stoke-on-Trent)

quite a lot to be learned from them and prices are not too high. 'Gaudy Welsh' tableware, which just scrapes in as lustre as it incorporates (though not too obviously) some pink/purple lustre among its strong enamel colours, is also usually around at fairs in abundance. Here, however, caution is needed for its production was carried on over a very long period from latish in the nineteenth to well into the twentieth century, notably by firms such as Charles Allerton of Longton in Staffordshire. Usually, but not always, Allerton pieces will be marked, but they will not be dated. Two-day fairs or longer tend to attract the more serious and better-quality dealer. Whether it be through visiting fairs or antiques shops, if a dealer becomes your friend and knows that you are a serious buyer, he may well reserve a piece for your inspection or even ring you up to ask if you are interested in something unusual he has found.

Restoration

Mention was made just now of the possibility of being offered a restored piece of lustreware. So much lustre decoration was carried out on pottery which, in relation to porcelain, is easily damaged, that it is not surprising that a good deal of what survives from the nineteenth century is either chipped or cracked. Small chips are not considered too serious a fault by the antiques trade or most collectors

and will not make a great deal of difference to the price though, as said earlier, a reputable dealer should always draw a customer's attention to them. Cracks are much more of a problem and, whereas a chip can easily be filled in by a competent restorer so that it more or less vanishes, a crack is infinitely more difficult to deal with.

There are two aspects to consider with regard to restoration of both chips and cracks which, in the final analysis, come down to personal choice, so that it is as well to know the pros and cons of each. The first aspect to consider is whether or not one should buy a restored piece at all. If it is something of great rarity the answer is probably yes, but if the restoration has been badly done, the answer must be no. Amateur restorers are often tempted to have a go and, if a piece has been broken, stick it together with the wrong sort of adhesive. This may not allow the parts to come properly together and, over a period, grease and dust will gather in the join, leaving a dark line. To get rid of this will probably mean calling in a professional restorer to break the piece afresh and start again. If the piece is interesting but not exceptional, restoration after buying, professionally done, is probably worth while. The dealer may agree to have it done for you, but remember that you will have to pay for it and, inevitably, the price will drop should you wish to sell it later. Many dealers do not believe in having restoration carried out before selling, preferring

Plate 36. *A matching Sunderland jug and mug decorated in purple lustre and enamel colours, the latter carrying the legend 'Success to the Coal Trade', a surprisingly rare sentiment considering coal mining was a staple industry of* the area. Jug and mug inscribed 'To William Dawson, 1829'.
(Norfolk Museums Service)

to leave any decision about it to the customer.

All the above applies in general terms equally to the restoration of any kind of pottery or porcelain, but another consideration arises with lustreware, which may remove the element of choice altogether. The film of metal, be it platinum or gold, that makes the lustre decoration on a pot, whether it is the main design or simply a border or trim, can never be properly restored. The fact that it would have to be re-fired, which would play havoc with the undamaged lustre, makes this impossible. Special metallic paints are employed by restorers over damaged lustre areas and though, if they are well applied, their use may not be immediately obvious, close inspection will very soon reveal the difference. All the lustre sparkle will be missing. Damaged jug spouts and rims are not infrequently touched up in this way, and a light brush with the finger along a suspect rim may detect a slight roughness which would never be there with a true lustre covering. All of this adds up to one thing: consider with even more care than usual the buying of a piece of lustreware that has its main damaged area on the lustred surface – err on the side of restraint!

Reproductions and fakes

It may well be considered that there is not a great deal of difference between these two and in one sense this is true.

Plate 37. *This copper lustre jug with two spouts and two handles might have been useful for an ambidextrous owner, but must otherwise be considered as an interesting novelty. Probably Staffordshire, c.1825.*

53

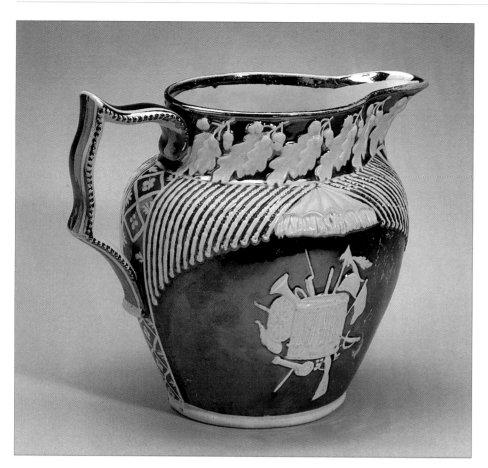

Colour Plates 41 and 42. *The figure on the side of this silver lustre-decorated, yellow-glaze jug has been variously described as the Duke of York and the Duke of Wellington, with the latter getting most votes. Exceptionally fine moulding is the outstanding feature here. The moulding on the reverse side of the same jug features military accoutrements. Probably Staffordshire, c.1815. Ht 5¼in: 146mm. (See also Colour Plate 31.)* (Gutman Collection)

Colour Plate 43. *Two very rare pink lustre and enamel decorated pearlware cats. Probably Staffordshire, their lightness in weight suggests an early date, perhaps 1810-1815. Hts 7¼in: 184mm and 6½in: 165mm. Sunderland cats have a similar pose but are over-all mottled lustre and have pug-like faces.*
(Gutman Collection)

Colour Plate 44. *A smaller than usual Sunderland pink lustre plaque featuring the Methodist preacher, John Wesley, who appeared on a number of Sunderland pieces. He toured the country during the second half of the 18th century and his influence was strong in the north-east for many years afterwards. c.1820. 6¾in: 171mm x 5¾in: 146mm.*

Plate 38. *One would expect to find the yellow-sailed galleon mark of A.E. Gray on the base of this jug. It has the typical Gray dark purple/pink mottled lustre and the heavily inked transfer print, in this case of The Shipwright's Arms. However, all one can truthfully say is that it is like the Gray products, from the turn of the century. Ht 5in: 127mm.*

Plate 39. *A reproduction resist lustre jug, probably from the early 1920s, with a very attractive, puce-coloured transfer print in the reserve. The comparatively heavy potting and handle shape were characteristic of a firm (possibly Adams) that supplied blanks for decorating to a number of companies, including that of A.E. Gray. The jug in Plate 38 is another example.*

The difference, however, must be based on the motive of the person or persons who produced them. If the intention is to deceive and make money out of something that is not genuine, that is one thing. If it is simply to copy something worthwhile from the past out of admiration for its design in order to perpetuate it, and there is a clear indication in the form of a factory or other mark to show that it is a copy, that is something else again. With lustreware there are plenty of both kinds about and also some where the motives of the manufacturer are by no means certain. For the collector who is just beginning, there are many traps one can fall into in this area, even with pieces made with the purist of motives.

One particular case has caused much controversy and it will be enlarged on in the section on the Leeds Pottery in Chapter 7. This was the work of James Wraith Senior early in the twentieth century, who justified his actions by insisting that he was simply continuing in the traditions of the old Leeds Pottery in which he had actually worked c.1865. He included typical Leeds flower holders, pierced plates, dishes and table decorations, figures and so on in his range, and the crazing that often occurred in his glaze could be disguised by over-all silver lustring, on occasions on pieces that were never so treated by the original factory. They are clearly marked LEEDS POTTERY, and some items attributable to Senior and bearing the Leeds mark are shown in Colour Plate 146.

Right at the other end of the scale and rather later in date is the lustreware produced by the the firm of A.E. Gray of Hanley in Staffordshire, referred to also in Chapter 10. Most of their decorative designs, many of which incorporated lustre, were entirely their own, and some of these, particularly those by Susie Cooper, were very fine; others, less so, for their output was variable. But the pieces with which we are here concerned are the range of Gray reproductions of Sunderland ware. These incorporated Sunderland style transfer prints, frequently the Shipwright's Arms in black and a genuine Sunderland rhyme on the reverse, all in a framework of mottled pink lustre. These were never sold as anything other than reproductions and carried the very distinctive Gray mark of a square-rigged or other type of ship, often in green and yellow, and the name of Gray and the words HAND PAINTED on the base. However, even with this, beginners who know nothing of Gray and the dates between which he was working can be misled into thinking they are much older than they are. To those who are familiar with the genuine thing, however, there are obvious differences. Jug handles, for instance, are usually much more typically Staffordshire (where they were made, of course) and not the loop type so typical of the East Coast firms; the transfer printing is usually heavier and darker on the Gray pieces and the lustre a harsher pink. If such a description makes sense, it could be described as being more 'metallic' looking. A.E. Gray himself regarded them as a tribute to the work of an earlier generation, which he much admired, and there is no reason to think that this sentiment was not genuine. I believe it is not unknown for an un-scrupulous dealer to grind away the Gray mark from the base of a jug or other item to trap the unwary buyer, but there is, in fact, a range of unmarked reproductions of Sunderland ware that closely resemble the Gray product, but that actually come from the north-east. They were made and marketed by Maling of Newcastle upon Tyne in the 1930s, a revival, they claimed, of the old traditions after a considerable gap.

Only experience and the handling of the real thing can really teach a collector what is genuine and what is not. All that can be done here is to show that all is not always what it seems and to sound a warning that everything one sees should not be accepted at its face value. Copper lustre is an area where a great deal of reproducing has taken place and, for that matter, probably still does. George Ray's famous Polka Jug design has been the most widely copied of all (by no means always in copper lustre though that is the most common) and must by now be thoroughly confused as to whom its ancestors really were. Wade, Beswick and Sandlands are among those who have produced copper lustre in comparatively recent times, using the old shapes and decorative designs. The Wade catalogue gives a considerable range of copper lustre jugs and other items, most of which are marked, but in any case their copper lustre has a distinctly bronze tint to it that distinguishes it from the really old.

Finally, in this admittedly brief review of some of the firms whose products can cause confusion and occasionally considerable resentment, if not rage, there is the Staffordshire firm of Adams. They produced in 1930 and marketed through Hill-Ouston, a Birmingham wholesaler, a range of

Plate 40. *Probably from the Staffordshire firm of Adams early this century, this pink splashed lustre jug features a coloured transfer print in the reserve. As the title beneath it states, it is of 'The Death of Punch', an episode from the series of Hogarth prints featuring Dr Syntax. Ht 5in: 127mm.*

Plate 41. *This late 19th or possibly early 20th century figurine purports to be by John Walton of Burslem which, if true, would date it from the 1820s. It even bears the familiar Walton scroll moulded on the back with his name on it but the lettering lacks serifs and the moulding is below Walton standard. The pink lustring is confined to the sheep and the lamb. Ht 6in: 183mm.*

Colour Plate 45. *Three examples from the very wide variety of moulded milk jugs (mainly small ones) put out by the potteries over quite a long period from the 1840s on. All were decorated with copper lustre, mainly used as a trim, and with enamel colours, though the buff slip used on so many of them was always predominant. The jug with the red rose decoration is from Maling of Newcastle and, c.1878, much later than the others, which are almost certainly Staffordshire. Hts 4½in: 114mm, 4½in: 114mm and 5½in: 140mm.*

ceramics under the heading in their catalogue of *Reproductions of Old Staffordshire Ware*. Transfer prints with an American interest indicated the market they were aiming at, but the oddest item of all in this catalogue, headed Staffordshire Pottery, was a large bowl listed as *Pattern E8587. Reproduction of Sunderland Lustre Ship Bowl*, 9⅜in x 5in, 21s (Plates 42 to 44). Transfer prints of Ship Caroline and the Shipwright's Arms adorned it and a wide band round the inside of the rim which appeared at first glance to be mottled pink lustre turned out to be mottled pink enamel.

Care of Lustre

Lustreware, particularly silver and pink, displayed *en masse* on shelves can bring even the dingiest room alive and will continue to do so with only an occasional light dusting. The metallic film from which the lustre is made up is incredibly thin and one should never attempt to polish it or clean it with even the mildest of abrasive cleaners. These would almost certainly damage the lustre, if not completely remove it. However, sometimes a new acquisition will be found to have a thin film of grime, and it can be brought back to pristine condition by a light sponging with water to which a drop or two of a

Colour Plate 46. *Four moulded jugs with pink lustre trim, not a set though two are similar, with each of the others showing a different variation of the* same basic strawberry vine design. Probably Staffordshire, c.1830-1840. Hts 7in: 178mm, 6in: 152mm, 6in: 152mm, and 8in: 203mm.

Plates 42, 43 and 44. *A reproduction Sunderland bowl featuring ship* Caroline *on the inside and* The Shipwright's Arms *on the outside. That it was intended by its makers (Adams) for the American market is evidenced by the additional eagle motif, though who the James Leech was is still puzzling researchers. The bowl was also distributed in the United Kingdom in the 1930s by wholesaler Hill Ouston of Birmingham at twenty-one shillings. What appear to be free brush strokes of pink lustre, and mottled pink lustre inside the rim, are actually carried out in pink enamel.*

mild detergent has been added. It is unlikely that anything more drastic than that will be needed.

Reference Books for the Collector

A fuller list of reference works appears in the Bibliography, but here are some comments on books of special interest for the collector of lustreware, one or two of which have already been mentioned.

As we know, a very small proportion of lustred items bears any maker's mark. Nevertheless there are some that do and these, if they do not actually give the company name, may need looking up. This can be a frustrating business as some firms had marks that varied with changes of ownership, not all of which can be found in the reference books. This is so, even with Dr Geoffrey Godden's massive *Encyclopedia of British Pottery and Porcelain Marks*, which is generally considered the last word. John Cushion's *Pocket Book of British Ceramic Marks* and Godden's *Handbook of British Pottery and Porcelain Marks* are alternatives and handier to carry around with you. These books, of course, cover all kinds of ceramics and are not confined to companies which produced lustred wares. The same can be said of the majority of general ceramic books. They are mostly either a review of quite a wide field which may well include lustreware, but only as one element, or else cover the work of one factory or possibly a group of manufacturers linked in some way. They can, however, if well done and comprehensively illustrated, be of great assistance to a lustre collector, for they show the styles and shapes, and the decorative schemes used by the various factories. These can help one to place an unmarked lustre piece by its similarity to a piece of unlustred ware shown in one of the books.

Books giving the origin of prints that have been used as transfers can be useful, too, though not necessarily in placing a ceramic pot with a particular factory. They may help with this but, if the date of the print is known, it should at least give a reasonable guide to the earliest possible date of the pot, and knowing the origin of a print on one of your pieces helps to round out the picture.

Other useful sources of information are those catalogues and pattern books put out by some of the nineteenth century potteries which have survived. For a number of these one must visit museums to see them, but others have been re-published in recent years with useful notes added. When it comes to books that specialise in lustreware they are, and always have been, few and far between. Even the Sunderland Museum's *Sunderland Pottery* does not deal purely with lustre, for the Wearside potteries produced a large quantity of other wares, many in their own way quite as distinctive as the lustre. As a matter of interest, Sunderland was a great producer of glass as well, and the original home of Pyrex.

A number of useful articles on lustreware by authorities such as Una des Fontaines have appeared and are still appearing from time to time in the *Newsletter* of The Northern Ceramic Society and I myself have contributed a few to *The Antique Dealer and Collectors Guide* and elsewhere, but otherwise writing on lustre has been sadly neglected.

Since its publication in the 1950s, W.D. John and Warren Baker's *Old English Lustre Pottery* has been considered the standard work on the subject. This is a large-format book full of photographs (not always of the highest quality) with some colour, and a text covering all the main producers of lustrewares. It is particularly good on Wedgwood, and on lustreware made for the American market, but the title of the book indicates a gap in its coverage of lustre. There is very little on lustred porcelains, which were an important element of the whole picture, and that great producer of lustreware, Davenport, gets only the briefest of mentions. *Old English Lustre Pottery* has long been out of print and is only obtainable second-hand. Nevertheless, it is reasonably easy to find and all serious lustre collectors should have a copy. True, later research has out-dated some of the information it contains and inevitably some questionable interpretations occur of facts that may still be in doubt today, but all in all it contains much valuable information.

Since 1991, however, a usurper has taken over its crown. Gibson and Godden's *Collecting Lustreware,* which is also of large format and far more comprehensive and up-to-date in its research than *Old English Lustre,* has now largely replaced the latter as a standard work. Lustred porcelains are fully covered and there is considerable technical detail on lustre recipes and techniques, not to be found elsewhere. And, once again, there are plenty of pictures to help the collector in identification.

Apart from these two, there are, at the time of writing, only two short introductions, the first of which is out of print. John Bedford's *Old English Lustre Ware* in only 66 pages tells one enough to whet one's appetite and my own small *Lustreware,* one of the Shire Books ceramic series, will, I believe, do the same. There is nothing, really, between these two extremes of large and small volumes, a gap, I hope, that this present book will fill.

A good many of the wares described and illustrated in these pages have been chosen because they represent the best or the most unusual of lustre-decorated items. Others have been picked because they are marked with their maker's name so that identification can be positive or else because, by their shape or decoration, they give a very good clue as to where they came from. The same general points could be made about lustreware on display in museums, so perhaps the samples shown in them and in this book could be said not to be completely representative of the whole. The emphasis is on the best, but in fact a great many items of an everyday nature are shown and discussed as well, in word and picture. Their decoration in most cases is extremely simple, a necessity for items produced in large quantities for use in the home and not for display in a show case, though this does not mean that they cannot be extremely attractive. They are likely to make up the bulk of what an enthusiast may find at the non-specialist antiques fairs and are an excellent starting point for any collection.

CHAPTER IV

Staffordshire

If only because it was the first in the field with lustreware, Staffordshire deserves to open this account of the many pottery producing areas that followed its lead in this particular skill. Another and equally good reason is that it was by far the largest and most influential. There were, during the peak period, a tremendous number of companies, large and small and sometimes tiny, producing lustreware in the six towns, Hanley, Burslem, Fenton, Longton, Tunstall and Stoke, which made up what became known as the Potteries.

Bordering Hanley to the north is the Cobridge district which, from the middle of the eighteenth century, was noted for the production of coloured enamels and as a centre for firms specialising in ceramic decoration. Burslem in its heyday was perhaps the grandest of the six towns and the names Enoch Wood, Wedgwood, Obadiah Sherratt and John Walton were prominent in its story. The third town, Fenton, was not associated with any of the greatest names in the story of lustre decoration, but two firms of note there were F. & R. Pratt and that of Miles Mason and his son Charles. Lane End, later to be known as Longton, was from early on a producer of coal to fire the bottle ovens of the Potteries, but in the nineteenth century also became a major producer of bone china. Hilditch and Aynsley are names associated with the area. Tunstall, the most northerly town, had a long history of brick and tile making, tiles still being a speciality of the area through the firm of Johnson-Richards. In the nineteenth century it was the home of the long succession of Adams families.

These six, as towns do, gradually expanded, absorbing the many small villages (a number with their own potworks) that surrounded them until, in 1910, against a certain amount of local opposition, it was decided that the time had come to amalgamate the six into one town under the name of Stoke-on-Trent.

Not all the Staffordshire firms were potters themselves, for some, like Bailey and Batkin, were supplied with blanks by other firms and carried out their lustring for them. This helped them to develop a prosperous business, but many others were not equally successful. A very large proportion of the firms were set up by men trained in the craft of pottery making, but not so skilled in running a business. Many of them over the years went into bankruptcy, and their stock and equipment was sold off by the assignee for what it would fetch. This included the copper plates for transfer printing, so that what at one time might have been

a transfer design exclusive to a certain manufacturer, by which he could be identified, ended up with someone completely different to the confusion of all. Sometimes it was not a question of bankruptcy but of being taken over, which would produce much the same result, or of the dissolving of a partnership and the bringing in of a new partner who could provide the capital needed to carry on. This might result in a change of name.

There was the almost inevitable copying of popular lines, not just by potteries in one area but between the areas themselves. Even so, the multiplicity of pot-works led to great diversity. This is one of the things which makes collecting lustreware such an exciting pastime, though the lack of makers' marks on practically all of their products also makes it one of great frustration. Excitement and frustration combined together make a heady mixture.

As well as being the first in the field, it can be said, I think, that the Staffordshire potters led the others in innovation. Where they showed the way, others followed and, while it may be difficult, for instance, to tell a Swansea piece decorated in the primitive, cottage style from one from the Potteries, it is more than likely that the Staffordshire design was the original. However, some manufacturers in other areas, such as the Leeds Pottery and probably Herculaneum in Liverpool, achieved a quality equal to if not exceeding that of Staffordshire at its best and showed originality in design. It can be said, too, that it was the potteries of the north-east, of Sunderland and Newcastle, that were the only ones that really went their own way in the lustre decoration of their pieces. More will be said about that in the accounts of the factories of the north-east in Chapter V.

The centres of ceramic production naturally sprang up in areas where clays suitable for potting could be found and extracted with the minimum of trouble. It was also advantageous if there were coalfields nearby to produce the fuel necessary for the pot ovens. Districts combining these two desirable qualities were fortunately in many cases near ports at the mouths of river estuaries and, as the export market made up a large proportion of the output of finished wares, this had considerable advantages. The large crates and hogsheads in which china and porcelain were packed could be loaded straight on to the ships, saving added transport costs. Of the lustre producing areas, Sunderland and Newcastle, on the Wear and Tyne respectively, Stockton and Middlesbrough further south on

Colour Plate 47. *Copper lustre jugs to this pattern, probably from the factory of Enoch Wood were decorated in many ways, of which this example is one of the most attractive. The coloured transfer print, which runs right round the jug, depicts the fruits of the earth (or possibly just the British empire as there is a large heraldic crown beneath the spout) and some of the people who inhabited it. c.1830-1835. Ht 6in: 152mm.*

Colour Plate 48. *This copper lustre loving cup, with its distinctive handle shape, and with its wide yellow banding and oval reserves containing finely executed bat prints of cows, matches the second jug closely, though the latter has a different pictorial theme, using enamel colours. If the jug in Plate 81 is by Enoch Wood, as seems almost certain, so will be this handsome loving cup. c.1830-1835. Hts 6½in: 165mm and 6in: 152mm.*

Colour Plate 49. *Two small milk jugs (ht 3in: 76mm) combining a multitude of decorative techniques. The smaller one has a pink lustre spout and inner rim, and a broad copper lustre band round the top with enamel flowers painted on it above a white band. The broader band round the centre of the body has a blue slip and is decorated in its turn with sprigging of enamel-coloured floral sprays. The foot is* in mottled pink lustre. In the larger jug, a second copper lustre band takes the place of the blue slip. Probably only Enoch Wood would have taken so much trouble on what was, to all intents and purposes, an item for everyday use rather than display. There are other indications, too, that these jugs came from the Wood factory (see Colour Plates 52 and 53). c.1820. Hts 4in: 102mm and 3¼in: 83mm.

Colour Plates 50 and 51. *A magnificent example of the pottery decorator's art. The yellow-glaze body has two enormous reserves, featuring on one side a mounted bugler and on the other a very strange shield featuring a riding boot and a shoe, with another shoe suspended in space above it. It has not proved* possible to place the unit to which the bugler belongs with certainty, but elements in his uniform indicate, according to The National Army Museum, either Artillery or Yeomanry Cavalry. The decoration on the neck, rim and handle is in pink lustre. c.1830. Ht 8in: 203mm.

Plates 45, 46 and 47. *A teapot, cup and saucer and slop basin from a teaset, c.1840. The pink lustre decoration is in a style used extensively by Allertons, but probably by others as well.*

the Tees, Liverpool on the Mersey, Swansea and Bristol, all had this advantage which the Stoke-on-Trent area and the Yorkshire potteries lacked (though Yorkshire did, in fact, use Hull). In the days before railways changed things dramatically, the Staffordshire potteries utilised narrow-boats on the Trent and Mersey Canal to carry their goods to Liverpool, whence there were frequent sailings of cargo ships to America and elsewhere. It was, in fact, a two-way arrangement, for the narrow-boats would come in the opposite direction from Liverpool, carrying white clays from Cornwall and Devon for use in porcelain production.

This, then, in outline, is the early industrial background of an area in the North Midlands which became the cradle of an industry that was to produce, and is still producing, some of the finest and most beautiful and sought-after ceramics in the world. The logical follow-up to this account is to have a more detailed look at some of the men and the companies that made it possible though, of necessity for this particular book, we are confined to those who made use of lustre decoration.

The Adams Family

The Adams family was one of the most famous Staffordshire families, being able to trace the line back to the fourteenth century. Later records show that they were established at Brick House, Burslem, in 1657 and John Adams is known to have been manufacturing black and mottled ware there in 1715. By the early part of the eighteenth century, three Adams cousins, confusingly all bearing the Christian name William, were operating separate potteries in what is now the Staffordshire area. Of the many businesses run by various members of the family over the years, these three were the most influential.

The eldest lived from 1746 to 1805. After working for a while for Josiah Wedgwood, he took over his father's factory at Burslem, also establishing one at Tunstall and the Greengates Pottery. He made blue jasperware in the Wedgwood pattern, matching it in quality, and also stonewares and creamware. His son, Benjamin Adams, succeeded him, carrying on the business until the early 1880s. His marks, when any were used, included ADAMS, ADAMS & CO., and W. ADAMS & CO.

The next William Adams (1748-1831)

Plate 48. *A pink lustre teapot, milk jug, sucrier and saucer from a miniature teaset impressed Davenport and produced by them c.1850. The decorative foliage is in green and chestnut red enamels.*

operated the Brick House works from 1769 and moved in 1774 to Cobridge. He specialised in blue transfer printed tableware and also had a limited production of pottery figures. There are no known marks.

The third William (1772-1829) was a son of Richard Adams of Cobridge, establishing his own firm in 1804 and, in due course, acquiring three more factories. Large quantities of transfer printed ware were made, much of it specifically designed for the American market. One of this Adams' sons opened a branch in New York to take care of distribution there and later, with three brothers, eventually took over his father's firm, continuing with the manufacture of earthenware for both the home and the overseas market. His marks included ADAMS, either impressed or printed, while for the American market there was an impressed eagle and the name of the design in a cartouche. Wares bearing the painted or stamped mark ADAMS EST 1657, TUNSTALL ENGLAND, are modern and date from the twentieth century.

A large and important firm such as Adams, continuing from generation to generation and with a number of different factories putting out both pottery and porcelain, must almost certainly have produced large quantities of lustreware from early in the nineteenth century. In support of this supposition an American invoice, dated 1837 and still in existence, lists Adams lustred wares which had been shipped from Liverpool to Philadelphia and there are other, though scanty, clues that lustre was, indeed, an important part of their output. Unmarked pieces of both pottery and porcelain have shapes and mouldings identical to others known, for one reason or another, to be from an Adams factory. At the time of writing (a necessary prefix to

so many statements concerned with ceramic research), few marked lustre-decorated pottery pieces are known and none at all in lustred porcelain.

The three nineteenth century Adams potteries mentioned above were those concerned in the most important period, though Adams companies, under varying styles, continued in production until well into the twentieth century. Some of their later work tended to look backwards. John and Baker, in *Old English Lustre Pottery* of 1951, have this to say: '…among their present day productions may be mentioned the items with coloured engravings from The Tour of Dr Syntax in Search of the Picturesque, in panels with a solid silver background.' So silver lustre was included in their output at this comparatively late date, but un-lustred (and unmarked) Dr Syntax jugs of about the same period were also made. At one time these jugs, with their coloured prints, were thought to have originated about 1820 at the Cobridge pottery of Ralph and James Clews but everything about them, not least the pottery itself, clearly indicates the twentieth century. The best-known print features the heartbreaking 'Death of Punch', an obviously much-loved white horse, shown in extremis *(Plate 40)*. Dr Syntax, according to Brewer's *Dictionary of Phrase and Fable,* was 'The pious, henpecked clergyman, very simple minded, but of excellent taste and scholarship, created by William Combe to accompany a series of coloured comic illustrations by Rowlandson. His adventures were told in eight-syllabled verse in *The Three Tours of Dr Syntax* (1812, 1820 and 1821)'.

In the 1930s Adams produced some mock Sunderland jugs and bowls complete with fairly genuine-looking

Colour Plate 52. *Enoch Wood at his best, this copper lustre jug with its sprigging of the white bull (which appears on both sides) is of highest quality. Under the spout the moulding is a combination of the English rose, the Scottish thistle, the Irish harp and something which could, stretching the imagination, be a Welsh dragon. All are surmounted by a crown, supported by two putti. c.1825-1835. Ht 7in: 178mm.*

Colour Plate 53. *Like the jug above, the general style and the floral decoration on copper lustre round the top form pretty firm clues that this large hunting jug is from Enoch Wood's factory, even though the modelling of the dogs is perhaps not up to his usual high standard. The huntsman himself is modelled under the spout and a fallen stag on the reverse. c.1825-1830. Ht 7in: 178mm.*

Colour Plate 54. *A very fine pottery jug, unmarked, but with the handle, blue slip and the sprigging very much in the Enoch Wood pattern. The pink lustre banding is so dark as to be almost copper. c.1820s. Ht 5in: 127mm.*

Colour Plate 55. *A pair of pink lustre-trimmed cream jugs, that on the left impressed WOOD & CALDWELL and that on the right ENOCH WOOD & SONS showing clearly how similar the products of the two companies could be. Fine coloured enamel sprigging is a feature of both. c.1810 and 1820. Hts 4½in: 114mm and 3½in: 89mm.*

Plates 49 and 49a. *An enormous (24in: 600mm) jug from Davenport, silver lustred all over, inside and out. Existing documentation in the Liverpool Museum shows that it was made to the order of an African chief to hold rum. The small picture gives a good idea of its size. c.1820.*
(The National Museums and Galleries of Merseyside, Liverpool Museum)

Plate 50. *A drabware jug with pink lustre on the fluted rim and handle. Transfer printed in black with the 'Muleteer' pattern. The mark on the base consists of a triangle with a centre dot in lustre and the name Davenport with an anchor, impressed. c.1835-1840. Ht 8in: 203mm.* (Blakey Collection)

Plate 51. *A beautifully decorated silver lustre-decorated bulb pot, c.1810-15. 5½in: 140mm. Probably Staffordshire.* (Gutman Collection)

transfer prints in black of the Farmers' Arms, and an American eagle, the latter giving a good idea of their intended market (Plates 42 to 44). The type of pottery used and the fact that what should have been broad pink lustre swirling brush strokes surrounding the transfer prints was carried out in pink enamel meant that all but the very inexperienced collector would not be fooled. Some of these wares carried the Adams name stamped in black on the base. In 1966 the Adams organisation was absorbed into the Wedgwood group of companies.

See Colour Plate 39 and Plates 39, 40, 42 to 44.

Allerton 1860-1942

The firm of Charles Allerton, Benjamin Brough and William Green of Longton, Lane End, was another one that continued, restructured from time to time, from its founding in the nineteenth century (1832) until well into

the twentieth. It would seem highly likely that they were the producers of more rather run of the mill lustred porcelain and pottery combined than any other manufacturer. Their range contained all three kinds, pink, copper and silver lustre, though it was not until comparatively late that they started using a factory mark so that identification could be positive. According to Dr. Geoffrey Godden, the mark 'Allertons Ltd' dates from 1912 when the style of the firm itself was changed to this. The word Allertons with or without a crown dates from 1912 onwards. Made in England was added after 1920.

Right until the end the company's designs changed very little and in the twentieth century they were using lustre decorative schemes that had been unaltered from earliest days. This can make it difficult for the uninitiated to sort out the old from the comparatively new, which is particularly unfortunate. There are today many odd cups

Plate 52. *A miniature settee, 3½in: 90mm high and 6in: 152mm long, and a pigeon-on-nest oval dish, 4½in: 114mm high by 6in: 152mm long. Both, except for the pigeon's head, which is white, are over-all lustred in silver. Possibly Staffordshire, c.1820.* (Gutman Collection)

69

Colour Plate 56. *A pair of jugs, slightly different in size, but both with a blue slip and the same dynamic sprigging of a mythical beast, the front half resembling a winged lion, on both sides, plus the same oak and acorn moulding round the top. The sprigging on the smaller jug is almost entirely decorated with pink lustre, which is unusual. Exact duplicates of the winged lion motif, together with the decorative sprigging under the spout of the larger jug, can be found on wares attributed to the Shorthose factory. c.1820. Hts 4½in:114mm and 5¼in: 133mm.*

Colour Plate 57. *An extremely fine set of three urn-shaped vases decorated with very dark purple lustre, each vase incorporating silhouettes of classical figures, every one different. Another similar set of three, also unmarked and with a different decorative scheme, is described as being of Davenport type in Gibson and Godden's* Collecting Lustreware, *which is about as close as one can get to the maker. c.1810. Hts 4in: 102mm, 4½in: 114mm and 5in: 127mm.*

Colour Plate 58. *A Staffordshire jug with a boldly moulded fruiting vine motif on either side. Pink lustre and green enamel have been used here, but the same jug appeared in a number of different decorative combinations. c.1815. Ht 5½in: 140mm.*

Colour Plate 59. *A porcelain pink lustre cup and saucer, the decoration of the speckle-breasted bird on both matching that on the jug in Colour Plate 72 c.1820s. Saucer dia 5¼in:133mm.*

Colour Plate 60. *A pink lustre, London shape, porcelain cup and saucer incorporating a design of great sophistication when compared to the primitive 'cottage' style. Staffordshire, c.1830. Saucer dia 5½in: 140mm.*

Plate 53. *Variously described as furniture supports or as being for use in holding open the sash windows common in the 19th century, nobody seems quite sure what these objects really were. They were usually modelled as portrait busts of celebrities or to resemble birds or animals. This pair,* *representing the heads and forepaws of lions have, in fact, almost human features and certainly most un-lion-like noses. Over-all silver lustre.*
(Courtesy, Winterthur Museum, from the Gutman Collection)

and saucers and even semi-complete tea services of obvious Allerton origin at antiques fairs at quite modest prices, but no way of knowing how old they are, which is a pity as they are just the sort of thing a beginner might go for.

Without being able to identify any positively, it is difficult to say what the Allerton silver lustre may have been like, but in general their pink lustre decoration was singularly uninspired. Their tea services could well be called bread and butter lines. At one time Allertons were advertising that they were prepared to re-lustre pieces that had become worn.

Allerton, Brough & Green (c.1832-59) became Allertons of the Park Works, High Street, Longton, from c.1860 to 1942. Marked Allerton lustrewares come from the twentieth century and the marks usually take the forms ALLERTONS LONGTON or ALLERTONS 1813, the latter surrounded by a scroll with Made in England below it.

See Plates 45 to 47.

Aynsley 1791-1809

There were two John Aynsleys involved in pottery and porcelain manufacture at Lane End in the 19th century. John Aynsley I was named as an enameller in 1790 and a pottery manufacturer in 1796 and 1802. He appears to have occupied his works until at least 1810, being

mentioned as a working potter in 1818 and an engraver in 1822. He died in 1829 and his obituary described him as 'introducer into Lane End of that description of ware called 'lustre'. Simeon Shaw, in his history of the Staffordshire Potteries said, as mentioned in Chapter 1, that John Aynsley introduced silver lustre in Lane End and, since 1804, it has 'been practiced, with varied success, through the whole of the district', the early date he gives indicating that he was writing from hearsay. Pottery survives today with engravings signed by John Aynsley I and is much sought after.

John Aynsley II was the grandson of John Aynsley I and worked in the pottery industry from the age of nine, being employed over the ensuing years by a number of companies and gaining a thorough grounding in his trade. Eventually, in 1857, he entered into a partnership with Samuel Bridgwood as a manufacturer of china, though no marked pieces are recorded. The partnership lasted until some time after 1865, but the business itself continues to the present day as Aynsley China.

Bailey & Batkin

Bailey and Batkin was the partnership formed in Longton in 1814 to carry on business as gilders, enamellers and lustrers of earthenware and china, William Bailey having been among the first to use lustre decoration. It was a highly successful union, which was said by their contemporary, William Ridgway, during the course of his evidence to a Select Committee of the House of Commons in 1816 proposing to limit the employment of children, to do nearly half of all the lustring in the Potteries.

Until the pioneering work carried out by Rodney Hampson and published under the title *Longton Potters 1700-1865,* which is Volume 14 of the *Journal of Ceramic History* published by the Potteries Museum, Hanley, Stoke-on-Trent, it was supposed that Bailey and Batkin were potters in their own right, as well as carrying out decoration for others. This idea was reinforced by the fact that a number of records still exist detailing orders from America for a wide range of ceramics, teasets, coffee pots, teapots, sugars and creams in both earthenware and china, much of it lustred. The truth is, however, as Mr. Hampson's researches revealed, that they 'bought in undecorated china and earthenware from other factories to enamel, gild or lustre', which they sold under their own name much as the firm of A.E. Gray was to do something like one hundred years later. It is possible, too, that some of the smaller potteries for which they carried out decoration lacked storage space for their finished products and were only too happy to let Bailey and Batkin carry out their overseas shipments.

In view of the extensive and varied nature of their work it seems a pity that so much emphasis has been put by writers in the past on the Bailey and Batkin 'Perdifume', which was patented in 1824 as 'Gas Consumer for consuming the smoke from gas burners and lamps'. It was probably because they were unique, and the fact that nobody was sure, until Rodney Hampson came up with the

Plate 54. *The Staffordshire firm of Dudson produced large quantities of these flask-shaped jugs, known, for obvious reasons, as 'tulip' jugs. Note the exceptionally deep exterior moulding of the flowers, highlighted with silver lustre. c.1830. Ht 7in: 178mm.*

answer, just what they were for, that so much attention was given to them. They had been described, variously, as wig stands, items to be used for advertising the company's wares and a number of other things but, though they were actually only one not very important item among many, they cannot be ignored in any account of the company's work.

They were strange and by no means beautiful objects,

Plates 55 and 56. *Two views of a commemorative jug, decorated especially for the American market and bearing the engraver's name, Bentley, Wear and Bourne, in running script directly under the engravings on each side. These illustrate American naval victories and show, respectively, the* Wasp *boarding the* Frolic *and the* Enterprise *capturing the British* Boxer. *They*

commemorate Commander Penny's victory on Lake Erie in 1813 and Commander Mcdonough's on Lake Champlain in 1814. The jug body is buff with a broad blue band and pink lustre trim. c.1820. Ht 5¼in: 133mm. Formerly in the McCawley collection of Liverpool jugs.

(Gutman Collection)

Colour Plate 61. *Two different decorative treatments of the ever-popular George Ray polka jug, the design registered by him on 11 April 1852, and widely copied by others over the years. The moulded, diamond-shaped registration mark on the bases of these jugs is indecipherable, indicating that they are almost certainly not original. Pink and copper lustre and enamel colours. c.1860. Ht 8in: 203mm.*

Colour Plate 62. *A particularly attractive pink lustre bone china cup and saucer, one of the multitude of designs put out by the Staffordshire potteries in the first half of the 19th century. Saucer dia 5½in: 140mm.*

Colour Plate 63. *A pottery saucer dish with a fruiting vine pink lustre decoration and yellow rim and banding. Possibly from Factory Z. c.1815. Dia 8in: 203mm.*

Colour Plate 64. *A pink lustre and enamel-decorated porcelain cup and saucer, the elaborate design possibly emanating from Factory Z. c.1825. Saucer dia 5½in: 140mm.*

Colour Plate 65. *This trio look to be typical examples of the earthenware jugs put out by countless manufacturers in the 19th century. That they are, in fact, in porcelain might indicate that they came from a pottery normally producing earthenware but venturing into the field of china production. The decoration combines pink lustre trim, coloured mouldings round the top, and coloured transfer prints of hunting scenes round the lower part of the body. c.1820s. Hts 4¼in: 108mm, 4in: 102mm, and 3¾in: 95mm.*

Plates 57 and 58. *Two more American commemoratives with engravings of Captain Jones of the* Macedonia *(war of 1812) and of George Washington. The following words frame Washington's head:* Gen WASHINGTON

Departed this life Dec 14th 1799 and the tears of the Nation watered his grave. There is also the following, 'Æ 67', which may possibly be a clue to the engraver. Pink lustre trim. Staffordshire c.1820s. (Gutman Collection)

Plate 59. *This jug features a decorative scheme used by many manufacturers, in particular by Davenport. It has an over-all pink lustre wash with a black transfer print superimposed on it, in this case of an oriental scene. Note, too, the swan neck handle. The printed mark on the base is E.C.& T., standing for Everard, Colclough and Townsend, a Longton, Staffordshire firm. c.1840. Ht 9in: 229mm.*

clearly made specially to order for Bailey and Batkin and then decorated in all-over silver lustre by them before being put on the retail market. They took the form of a ball or globe, mounted usually, though not always, on a tall, conical base and surmounted by a crouching lion. The heights of the different models varied from 8½in (216mm) to 14in (356mm) and there was a moulded band round the centre line of each globe into which the words BAILEY & BATKIN, SOLE PATENTEES were worked. It is difficult to see how they could have been suspended over gas burners or lamps as there is no obvious means of attachment for a cord or chain. There seems to be no record of how successful they were or how many were actually sold, but they are a scarce item nowadays and it would seem probable that they were not a very successful line.

The partnership of Bailey and Batkin was dissolved in 1826 and their works passed into other hands.

Bentley, Wear & Bourne c.1813-23
William Bentley, William Wear and Samuel Bourne of Vine Street, Shelton, were decorators who carried out work of high quality for others. They specialised in transfer prints and enamelling, many of their designs being aimed at the American market. The engraving for their series of jugs illustrating Anglo-American naval engagements is particularly fine (Plates 55 and 56) and some at least of their prints are signed Bentley, Wear & Bourne, Engravers and Printers, Shelton, Staffordshire. Many of the pieces they decorated carried lustre trim, so it seems certain that they must have carried out this kind of work as well.

Copeland & Garrett 1833-1847 – *see* Spode

Cyples 1784-1848

Rodney Hampson lists no fewer than nine different individuals or partnerships incorporating the family name of Cyples as occupying the Market Street works (later to be known as Cyples Old Pottery) in Longton during the sixty-four years between 1784 and 1848. It seems likely that the company, under the names of William and Richard Cyples, who took over the running of the business from their parents c.1833, did produce lustre decorated pottery and porcelain and that this was continued until the end of the final partnership of William Cyples and George Barker in 1848.

See Colour Plate 81.

Henry Daniel

A highly talented and enormously influential figure in the story of ceramic decoration, particularly of porcelain, Henry Daniel, was, until 1806, in partnership with John Brown, and undoubtedly much involved in the early story of lustre. One of their employees, John Hancock (Colour Plate 1), was, as we have seen in Chapter 1, credited as being the first person to use it successfully.

Though in business independently, their workshops were actually within the premises of the Spode factory and, as enamellers and gilders, the arrangement was that they should carry out the decoration of much of Spode's fine china. Recipes for lustre appear in their records and certain Spode wares have silver lustre trim. Then came the variegated lustre enlarged on later in this chapter under the Spode heading and also in Chapter 3. Lustre, however, would appear to have played a comparatively small part in the output of Daniel and Brown or of Henry Daniel after this first partnership dissolved in 1806. After decorating within the Spode works, Daniel manufactured in his own name, but there is no evidence that he produced lustred wares.

Davenport 1794-1887

In the year 1794 George Davenport purchased the Unicorn Pottery at Longport to form what was to become one of the most important manufacturers of both pottery and porcelain in the history of British ceramics. At first earthenware only was produced, but by the beginning of the nineteenth century porcelain had become an even more important part of their output. So good was its quality that when the Prince of Wales visited the Potteries in 1806 the Davenport factory was one of three (the others being

Plate 60. *A most unusual silver resist lustre combined tobacco jar and candle holder, inscribed Thomas Smith 1815. It also incorporates a holder for snuff. Ht 8in: 203mm.*

(Gutman Collection)

Plate 61. *This jug, with its 'pineapple' moulding and decorated in silver lustre and red enamel, bears the impressed mark HARLEY, which would date it between 1805 and 1815. Ht 5in: 127mm. It should be compared with the jug from Job Meigh in Plates 17 and 18.*

Colour Plate 66. *A fine example of the work of Thomas Lakin, a drabware chestnut basket and stand decorated with silver lustre, both pieces impressed with the maker's name. c.1810-1817. Stand 11in: 279mm x 8¼in: 210mm.*

Colour Plate 67. *A Staffordshire jug using an enamel-coloured transfer print of a familiar chinoiserie theme over a pink slip, a very unusual combination, particularly taken in combination with the broad silver lustre banding and handle. Harley has been suggested as a possible manufacturer. c.1810. Ht 6½in: 165mm.*

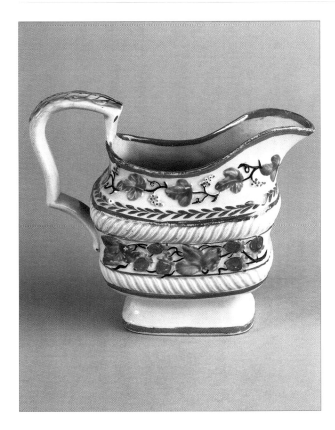

Colour Plate 68. *An attractive moulded pearlware cream jug, decorated in pink lustre and enamel colours, and of a shape more usually associated with black basalt wares. Probably Staffordshire, c.1820s. Ht 4½in: 114mm (to handle top).*

Colour Plate 69. *A jug in silver resist lustre on a mauvish-pink slip ground, quite heavily potted and probably from the second half of the 19th century, say 1860. Staffordshire. Ht 5½in: 140mm.*

Colour Plate 70. *A striking silver resist jug, yellow-glazed inside and out. The bird decoration might suggest Leeds, but is the handle right for that Yorkshire pottery? c.1820s. Ht 6½in: 165mm.*

Plate 62. *A pink lustre dish from a dessert service with the impressed mark of Thomas Lakin. c.1805-10.* *(Gutman Collection)*

tulips and has, not surprisingly, led to them being called Tulip Jugs. Quite a number have silver lustre decoration, but it should be pointed out that other manufacturers produced very similar jugs.

Everard, Colclough & Townsend 1837-1845
George Everard worked with a succession of partners at the potworks in Chancery Lane, Longton, the partners' names being incorporated into the title of the company alongside that of the founder each time a change of ownership was made. It is thought that both pottery and porcelain was produced and that the firm operated as decorators as well as potters. Though records show that lustreware was manufactured, the only tangible evidence is the jug shown in Plate 59. This has an over-all wash of pink lustre backing the transfer print design and has the mark E.C. & T. stamped on the base. The firm is recorded in the Great Exhibition Catalogue (1851) as exhibiting lustre.

Gibson & Sons 1884-1970
This company carried the Gibson name stamped on the base. They operated from the Harvey and Albany Potteries in Burslem from 1884 to 1970 and became one of the largest manufacturers of earthenware teapots in the world, but their products were aimed at the cheaper end of the market and showed a certain coarseness in the design and execution. A number of the teapots and other domestic wares had lustre decoration, many with an over-all silver lustre treatment (Colour Plate 156). Some designs reflected those of an earlier era.

Spode and Wedgwood) chosen for a special visit. The prince is known to have compared what he saw with the work of the Sèvres factory in France, and invoices for purchases he made still exist and include both porcelain and earthenware decorated with lustre.

Until the 1850s at least, Davenport were certainly one of the largest producers of lustreware, predominantly pink combined with enamel work, though they were among the first to use silver lustre. Documentary evidence shows that porcelain was included but Davenport did not mark his early porcelain. However, a great deal of lustred Davenport earthenware can be found today, very clearly marked with the firm's name in combination with an anchor.

See Colour Plates 57, 83 and 92 and Plates 48 to 50.

Dudson c.1800 to present day
One of the few firms dating from as early as 1800 to be still in production. Company records, incorporating recipes, show that Dudson lustreware was produced in respectable quantities, but it is unfortunate that it appears to have been unmarked. No one has as yet found a marked piece, but company historian, Audrey M. Dudson, in her book *Dudson, a Family of Potters Since 1800,* identifies as a Dudson design a certain moulded jug of which quite a number are still around (Plate 54). The prominent moulding on the sides of this incorporates

Plate 63. *A dish in a typical Lakin shape, which would identify it even if it were not impressed with the maker's surname. It is decorated in pink lustre with the foliage and berries in green and red enamel. The transfer print, intended to attract the American market, is in black, as opposed to the more usual Lakin blue. Captain Hull of the* Constitution *was an American commander in the war of 1812. c.1813-17.* *(Blakey Collection)*

Plates 64 and 65. *An American commemorative 'Jefferson' jug, bearing under the American eagle the following words:* Peace, Commerce and honesty, Friendship with all Nations – Entangling Alliances with none. Jefferson. *The design shown on the side of the jugs is obviously dedicated to* education for, reading downwards, each of the circular steps bears an appropriate *word:* ASTRONOMY, MUSIC, GEOMETRY, ARITHMETIC, LOGIC, RHETORIC *and* GRAMMAR. *Staffordshire, c.1826.*

(Gutman Collection)

Thomas Harley c. 1805-1808

The name Harley would automatically spring to the mind of anyone with a basic knowledge of lustreware seeing a pineapple moulded pottery jug (Plate 61) – and they could well be right, for this form of moulding was a speciality of Thomas Harley who was in business on his own at Lane End, Longton, for a very short period from 1805 until 1808 before he joined forces with another potter under the company name of Harley & Seckerson

The pineapple moulding was not exclusive to Harley, being used also by Charles Meigh and others, but it became very much his trade mark. A considerable number of the factory's wares were impressed with the single word HARLEY, though by no means all of them, so that identification cannot always be completely positive.

Sometimes the diamond-shaped segments of the moulding are picked out in different colours. Jugs decorated in this way were known as harlequin jugs and are much sought after. Others have a brown body and are in all-over silver lustre, but perhaps the commonest Harley jugs are in the natural colour of creamware on which has been carried out a very detailed floral design in silver lustre and chestnut red. An almost identical design appears on a number of Meigh pineapple jugs and it seems possible that the same outside decorator may have been employed by both firms. One wonders, however, why this particular design was chosen for either of them as it would look so much better on a smooth surface.

Domestic wares other than jugs were also made.

See Colour Plates 67 and 91 and Plates 29 and 61.

Thomas Lakin 1810-1817

Both as a potter and as a decorator, Thomas Lakin, though perhaps not quite reaching the highest levels in either field, nevertheless produced many wares of great charm and was an extremely important figure in the story of lustreware. This is because the facts about his work in the Potteries are

Plate 66. *A good example of a jug decorated with a painting in enamels rather than the more usual coloured transfer print, a process less suited to mass production but creating delightful results. The lustre trim is pink/purple. Probably Staffordshire. c.1820s.* *(Brighton Museum and Art Gallery)*

Colour Plate 71. *It has proved difficult to place this milk jug with a manufacturer as its elegant shape and slender base appear (at the time of writing) to be unique, though it has been suggested that one or other of the north-eastern potteries might have made it. The decoration combines copper lustre banding, a pink lustre spout and handle decoration, and enamel floral decoration executed with considerable élan. c.1820s. Ht 5in: 127mm.*

Colour Plate 72. *A Staffordshire pink lustre jug decorated in what one might call 'advanced cottage' style, probably carried out by an adult hand rather than a child worker. This bird, with its speckled breast, appears on a number of pieces (see Colour Plate 59), probably all from the same factory. c.1820s. Ht 6in: 152mm.*

Colour Plate 73. *Of oval section, the extreme lightness of this jug suggests an early date, say c.1815. Pink lustre is used only on the rim and round the foot. Enamel colours decorate the sprigging, which shows a hunt scene also found on a great many Staffordshire jugs and pots, indicating at least the area, if not the factory, in which this one was made. Ht 5½in: 139mm.*

Colour Plate 74. *Moulded hen-on-nest pottery baskets are by no means rare, but when decorated in pink lustre, as this one is, are less common. On this one there are also traces of green, over-glaze enamel, but most has been rubbed away. c.1830. Length of basket 6½in: 165mm.*

Colour Plate 75. *A rare pair of G. and C. Mason ironstone vases, decorated in their traditional style but with purple lustre on the rims, handles and around the base. Lustred Mason wares are far from common. These date from c.1835. Ht 8¼in: 210mm.*

Plate 67. *A selection of pink lustre cups and saucers in both pottery and porcelain, c.1820-30, showing just a few of the almost limitless range of* decorative schemes. These make teaware items like this a most attractive proposition for collectors.

Plate 68. *These moulded dogs, usually sold in pairs, were made in many sizes, large (13½in: 379mm) ones, as shown here, to stand at either side of the hearth, and smaller ones for the chimney piece. They were made in both Staffordshire and the north-east in enormous numbers and, though the upright stance was almost always the same, they differed in detail. Enamel colours were used for the nose and eyes and the highlights of the fur and the collar and chain were picked out either in gold or in copper or pink lustre. Alternatively they may have had chestnut red or black patches on their coats. Reproductions are still being made today, though they are usually quite easy to tell from the genuine article.*

now well documented and quite a large number of the lustred items, for which he was responsible in his role as a potter, are impressed with his name so that one has a better than usual idea of the range of his work. In addition, as described in Chapter 2, his widow published a book of his 'Valuable Receipts', which included his preparation of lustre and notes on his methods of working to help her to make ends meet after his death. She rather endearingly, though optimistically in view of her contemporaries' quite shameless copying of each others' ideas, added a plea that anyone wanting to use the information in the book should actually buy it and not make do with someone else's copy.

In the early 1790s Lakin was working in partnership with John Poole in Burslem, under the company name of Lakin & Poole, and then for a period set up on his own before working for the Longport firm of Davenport at the very end of the century. Within a few years the secret of the successful application of metals to ceramic bodies by lustring was becoming ever more widely known and Davenport was among the first in the field. Although he was employed in Davenport's glass works, it was probably during his time with them that Lakin first learned the technique and, as he stayed with the firm until 1810, he had plenty of opportunity to become familiar with all that was involved. At any rate, by that year he obviously felt confident enough to branch

Plate 69. *A pair of jugs in the style generally attributed to the Shorthose factory. The copper lustre is particularly deep and rich, with the white sprigging featuring classical themes making a striking and attractive contrast. The band inside the rims and some lining on the jug handles is in pink lustre. c.1810. Hts 5in: 127mm and 4in: 102mm.*

out once more, not quite on his own but in a very short-lived partnership in Stoke with William Arrowsmith, trading as Thomas Lakin & Co.

After that, going solo once again, there came a downward turn in his fortunes and research by Harold Blakey has shown that he was decorating for other manufacturers. In 1818 or 1819 he was appointed as a manager at the Leeds factory of Hartley Greens & Co., and clearly his experience in lustre decoration must have been of great value to a company which had produced over a number of years a wide range of lustred ceramics, among them jugs decorated with very high quality silver resist.

Thomas Lakin died in 1821 at the comparatively early age of fifty-one. The range of his decoration on a limited number of shapes was considerable, and many of his designs showed an innovative mind. Quite a number of them will be found illustrated in this book. As indicated by Harold Blakey, it is possible to make a distinction between Lakin's deep pink true lustre and the deep mulberry that we see on his white slip decoration, the latter being probably non-lustrous (no metallic film formed).

See Colour Plate 66 and Plates 62 and 63.

Job and Charles Meigh 1802-1860

From 1802 to 1832 Job Meigh, having dissolved an earlier partnership, operated from the Old Hall Pottery, Hanley. A

Plate 70. *A considerable rarity, this pink lustre plate bears the impressed mark JOSEPH STUBBS, LONGPORT contained in a circle with a leaf in the centre. c.1825. Dia 7in: 178mm.*
(Gutman Collection)

Colour Plate 76. *A flat-back bough or bulb pot decorated with two country scenes of fishing and one of ploughing in pink lustre on a buff ground. Bough pots, for holding flowers or bulbs, were made by many potteries, basically similar in design but with many different decorative schemes carried out in both silver and copper lustre as well as pink. Often nowadays the lid will be missing. Staffordshire. c.1820. Ht 6½in: 165mm and width 8in: 203mm.*

Colour Plate 77. *Quintal flower vases like this appeared from a number of potteries, both from Staffordshire and the north-east. The decoration and type of lustre varied from factory to factory. This one is difficult to place with any certainty with its combination of pink lustre on the rims and base and attractive blend of lustre and enamel colours on the main body. c.1820s. Ht 7½in: 191mm.*

Colour Plate 78. *A beautifully decorated pair of pink lustre vases, the combination of the lustre on both the blue and the white ground being particularly striking. Similar vases are shown in John and Baker's* English Lustre Pottery *but they are more squat in shape and thus less elegant. One of them has a lid, so it may be that this pair should have lids too. Probably Staffordshire. c.1820-1825. Ht 9in: 229mm.*

Colour Plate 79. *A very elegant coffee pot, pink lustre on a buff ground, in design reflecting the silverware of the period. c.1820. Ht 10¾in: 273mm.*

Plate 71. *A very popular design of moulded jug from around 1840-1860, the decoration accentuated with pink lustre and enamel colours. When the moulding is good, not by any means always the case, the words EPSOM CUP can be made out beneath the two stags.*

pineapple moulded jug dated 1808 in the style already described in the entry for Thomas Harley (Plate 61) bears the impressed mark MEIGH (Plates 17 and 18) and an earthenware teapot illustrated in *Anthology of British Teapots* by Miller and Berthoud are among the few pieces that can confidently be attributed to Job Meigh during these early years of the century. Both have silver lustre decoration.

Job Meigh died in 1817, leaving the business jointly to his widow and son Charles, but in 1832 they dissolved their partnership and Charles continued the business trading in his own name, still operating from the Old Hall Pottery. Some of his best-known creations were the extravagantly moulded stoneware Apostle jugs which became

Plate 72. *A rare pair of egg-cups with silver lustre rims and banding and pictorial designs in sepia on a white ground. c.1825. Ht 2in: 51mm.*
(Gutman Collection)

enormously popular. The figure of an apostle was moulded into each of twelve panels that made up the sides, and the Godden Collection in Worthing contains an example silver lustred over-all, though this is unusual. The mark C. MEIGH was substituted for the surname alone during the son's period, which ended c.1860, though the absence of marks on Meigh products in general makes it difficult to assess just how extensive was their lustring operation.

George Ray 1846-c.1860

George Ray is included here not because of the multiplicity of his lustred products but because he was the creator of one of the most popular relief-moulded jug patterns of the nineteenth century on which lustre decoration was frequently featured. Ray was primarily a modeller and, in 1852 and 1854, from his address in Drury Street, Longton, he registered two designs for moulded jugs, one of which was to become known as the Polka Jug. This featured a gaily-costumed couple dancing the polka and so great were the numbers produced that even today a polka jug can be picked up at almost any antiques fair at a very reasonable price. The design was quickly copied by other companies, decorated in many different ways. The most attractive had the dancers themselves in brightly-coloured enamels on a white glaze and surrounded by various decorative motifs, often in pink lustre. However, perhaps most numerous of all are those in over-all copper lustre and, judging by the number still about, production of polka jugs appears to be going on even today. One can buy them, as it were, hot from the kiln, but many of them are crudely made and poorly lustred. The moulds from which they are fashioned are clearly long past their useful life.

A distinguishing mark of genuine George Ray jugs should be the diamond registration mark moulded into the base, but later makers have clearly used a finished Ray jug to make their own moulds, including the registration mark, so it rarely means what it should (Colour Plate 61). Some quite high quality polka jugs have had the registration mark completely removed, though it is difficult to see why. The other Ray relief-moulded jug design dating from the early 1850s showed birds feeding their young in a nest. It seems certain that a number of other jugs of a similar nature can also be attributed to this potter.

John Shorthose 1815-1823

In the partnership of Shorthose & Heath, John Shorthose operated a pottery in Tontine Street, Shelton, from 1794 until 1815 and it is likely that, during the last few years of this joint venture, some lustred wares were produced. From 1815 onwards John Shorthose was on his own, continuing to run the Shelton pottery but also operating two more in Hanley, trading as Shorthose & Co. and obviously in a considerable way of business as a manufacturer of a wide range of earthenware goods. Examples impressed SHORTHOSE exist, such as the jug from the Pulver Collection shown on p. 151 of *Collecting Lustreware*, and the same collection also possesses an impressed Shorthose coffee pot. Then there is a range of jugs, very distinctive, which John and Baker attribute to this particular maker on the strength of a closely matching marked cup and saucer, though none of the jugs themselves appears to have borne a mark. They come in many sizes and examples are shown in Plate 69. All are coated with a particularly richly-coloured copper lustre, which forms a vividly contrasting background to white sprigging and banding. The sprigging combines vaguely heraldic designs and, usually, mouldings of putti cavorting in the altogether, as seems to have been their wont, in and around small chariots drawn by goats, while some of the bolder (or more foolhardy) spirits ride astride lions.

For reasons about which little is known, John Shorthose's prosperity did not last. His business appears to have dwindled and he was declared bankrupt in 1823, yet another of the many potters to follow this path in what, on the face of it, was a thriving industry.

Sampson Smith (Ltd.) 1851-1963

From its beginning in 1851 this company, which continued to trade until well into the twentieth century, is primarily famous for a wide range of large, moulded 'flat-back' earthenware chimney ornaments, many depicting military figures on horseback, with the highlights of the moulding gilded or else picked out in copper or pink lustre. Equally well known are their Staffordshire dogs (so-called though they were made elsewhere as well) which were manufactured in their thousands, some with enamel colouring and others with their highlights picked out in the same way as the flat-backs. Produced in pairs, the smaller ones would serve as chimney ornaments and the larger, 12in (305mm) or more high (Plate 68), would stand one each side of the hearth. They date from about 1820 onwards and such is the continuing demand that they are being reproduced to this day, though not by the original makers. Even in the early days Sampson Smith was by no means the only manufacturer of flat-back ornaments or of moulded dogs and, since few, if any, were marked, it is virtually impossible to sort out the products of one maker from the other.

Apart from these fireside ornaments, according to Dr. Godden, 'by 1864 Sampson Smith appeared in directories as producing enamelled china, gold and silver lustres in great variety'. Silver lustre teapots were an important line, but few pieces from this factory bear any sort of mark.

Plates 73 and 74. *Two views of a very large and impressive jug with rose-decorated, purple lustre neck and handle. The castle and its landscape setting are very finely painted with browns and greens as the predominant colours, and it seems strange that there is no clue as to the jug's origin. Note that, due to its size, it needed an extra hand-grip under the spout to assist in pouring. Probably c.1820-30.* (Brighton Museum and Art Gallery)

Colour Plate 80. *Looking every inch a pottery piece, this sucrier is, in fact, in bone china. The decoration in pink lustre and enamel colours can best be described as cheerful. Staffordshire, c.1820s. Ht 5½in: 140mm.*

Colour Plate 81. *A very handsome, pink lustre-decorated porcelain sucrier. The shape of the handle suggests that one of the Cyples companies of Lane End, Longton, might have been the manufacturer, but it is unmarked. c.1820s-1830s. Ht 6in: 152mm, width (including handles) 9½in: 241mm.*

Colour Plate 82. *A porcelain sucrier with very distinctive finial and animal head handles. The numerous sprays of flowers that constitute the main decoration are in enamel colours, some with pink lustre leaves. Pink lustre touches also appear elsewhere. Probably Staffordshire, c.1820-1830. Ht 6½in: 165mm.*

Colour Plate 83. *Bearing the imprint of Davenport on its base this jug, in pink lustre, was of a design produced by the factory in large quantities and a variety of decorative schemes. c.1835. Ht 6½in: 165mm.*

Plates 75 and 76. *Two sides of the same mug with unusually fine transfer prints in black on a pale buff body. The lustre is an unusual leaden colour. Possibly Herculaneum. Ht 4½in: 114mm.* (Blakey Collection)

Spode and his Successors (c.1784–1847)

In the second half of the eighteenth century, Josiah Spode was joined by his son, Josiah Spode II, who was to run the London showroom for the wares produced by the family pottery in Stoke. In 1797 Josiah died, Josiah II returned north to take over the running of the business, and it was after that time that the close association that was to develop

Plate 77. *A pink lustre saucer-dish with 'cottage'-style decoration of a kind made in huge quantities by potteries in Staffordshire and most other northern ceramic centres over a long period from the 1820s on. Sizes varied but this one is 8in: 203mm in diameter.*

between the Spode and the Copeland families began. After the death of Josiah II in 1827, and not long afterwards of his son, Josiah III, the Spode family decided to sell the business to William Taylor Copeland who, with his partner Thomas Garrett, traded as Copeland & Garrett, though they had the good sense still to make use of the prestigious Spode name. However, it does not appear that lustreware was a major item in this firm's products.

The important part played by the Spode factory in Stoke in the story of lustre decoration has already been recounted in Chapter I, and the work of John Hancock in the independent workshops of Daniel and Brown within the Spode property boundaries described, at least in outline (see Colour Plate 1). The Spode lustre that we know of was applied to standard Spode shapes in broad bands, framed in quite elaborate gilding, and much more nearly resembles steel than platinum. It is darker than the latter and appears dull in comparison but was, nevertheless, a great novelty in its time. Clearly the lustre element was still in the experimental stage and had yet to develop the glistening brightness that platinum lustring at its best can give. It would seem that experimental work in gold lustring was also going on at the same time, using added tin for purple lustre, and, from about 1810 onwards, the Daniel workshops were producing splashed lustre on shapes taken direct from Wedgwood patterns. The manager of Wedgwood's London showroom reported at the end of 1812: '…there is no doubt that Mr Spode will immediately begin to make them. I do not know how it is he gets up every new thing we have, almost directly. He has got our Variegated Lustre Nautilus hanging flower pots which he sells at 8/-, our price is 11/-...He also has the Dessert set Variegated Lustre wreathed shells and I almost think that he must get patterns from Etruria.' No invoking of the law, it will be noticed, to prevent this trespass into Wedgwood preserves simply because there was no law to invoke.

The quality of the Spode wares was as high as Wedgwood so that they could not be dismissed as cheap imitations. At least Spode had the grace to impress a number of them with their own name, which is more than was done by the majority of Wedgwood imitators. But, apart from these transgressions, Spode was one of the leading firms of its day and produced much fine bone china with its decoration of the highest standard and completely original.

Wedgwood 1797 to the present day
Probably the firm of Wedgwood is the best known of all the Staffordshire potteries. Mention its name and everyone will know (more or less) what you are talking about, even if they do not know how to spell Wedgwood. There can be little doubt that this pre-eminence was deserved for, going back to long before the coming of lustre decoration, the company, under the first Josiah Wedgwood, was an innovator and leader of the industry in the development of new ideas. He was the creator of a superior form of creamware which he called Queensware, much copied by others, and also of jasperware.

Lustre arrived on the scene after the death of Josiah in 1795, when his son, Josiah II, in partnership with his brother Thomas and cousin Thomas Byerley, took over. They were among the first to use it.

Plate 78. *A handsome Wedgwood pot-pourri vase in variegated lustre, c.1815-20.*
(Courtesy, Winterthur Museum, from the Gutman Collection)

In 1823, Josiah II's son, Josiah Wedgwood III, came in as a partner. That this firm is still going today as a flourishing concern with the highest standards is tribute to the fact that it was always a rarity among the nineteenth century manufacturers, a company with a good product that, despite periodic ups and downs, was also, in the long run, efficiently managed.

Wedgwood produced a certain amount of early silver lustre, sometimes with the over-all treatment and sometimes with a resist pattern. This was confined to the smaller domestic items such as plates, sugar basins, teapots, coffee pots and cups and saucers.

Old English Lustre Pottery illustrates 'a gold lustre pastille burner' and other items with the impressed mark JOSIAH

WEDGWOOD accompanied by the incised FEBY 2d 1805, so clearly, if this date can be taken at its face value, the company had lost no time in adopting the new technique.

However, it is for their variegated lustre from about 1810 onwards that Wedgwood is best known. A description of this is given in Chapter II, and it was used on a wide variety of individual items. Perhaps its most striking manifestation was on dishes moulded to resemble nautilus and scallop shells, which made up whole dessert services. The firm of Wedgwood is, of course, still a force to be reckoned with. In the twentieth century their Fairyland Lustre (see Chapter II) has been the outstanding feature (see Colour Plate 158).

See also Plates 5, 10, 78, 140, 141 and 143.

Colour Plate 84. *Two other versions of the pink lustre-trimmed jug shown in Colour Plate 19. These ones have bat prints of deer, a different one on each side. c.1820. Hts 5¼in: 133mm.*

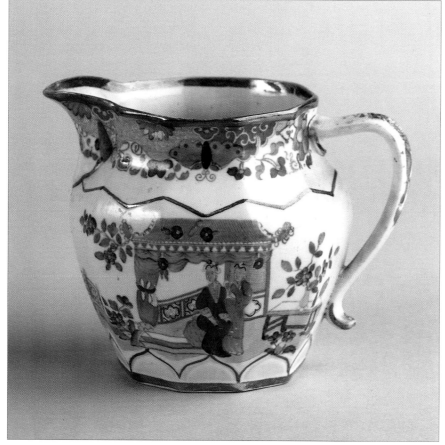

Colour Plate 85. *An unusual jug, in porcelain rather than pottery, decorated with a coppery-pink lustre trim and an oriental-style pavilion in enamel colours. c.1820s. Ht 4in: 102mm.*

Colour Plate 86. *Giving, from its potting, every impression of being earthenware, this pink, resist lustre coffee pot is, in fact, porcelain. The attempt to add realistic red strawberries to the resist depiction of a strawberry vine can hardly be said to be successful. Probably Staffordshire, c.1830. Ht 8½in: 216mm.*

Colour Plate 87. *A hound's head stirrup cup and a quite elaborate egg cup stand, both in mottled pink lustre. John and Baker show a similar stand in over-all silver lustre, attributed to Staffordshire, c.1810-1815.*
(Gutman Collection)

Plate 79. *Impressed WILSON, this beautiful pair of of ice-pails, complete with covers, have gilding over a rich copper lustre background with figures from Greek mythology in a frieze round the main body. c.1805-1810. Ht 10¼in: 260mm.*
(Gutman Collection)

Plate 80. *Even if this flowerpot were not impressed WOOD AND CALDWELL the distinctive light blue of the body with its brightly-coloured sprigged frieze would be a give-away. Here the dish in which it would normally be placed to catch excess water has been inverted to form a stand. Pink lustre is used for the trim and highlights. c.1818-1825. Ht 4½in: 114mm.*
(Gutman Collection)

David Wilson 1801–1807

Though founded in the eighteenth century by other owners, by 1801 the Wilson Church Works Pottery in Hanley had been in business for a number of years under the general managership of Robert Wilson, producing, with the help of his younger brother, David, high quality earthenwares and perhaps a certain amount of porcelain. In 1801, Robert died and David continued on his own, eventually being joined by his sons, the company becoming David Wilson & Sons. It is known that the Wilsons produced some silver lustre, but their speciality was a very handsome range of beautifully potted, brown-bodied wares with an over-all copper lustre ground often decorated with gilt Greek key borders and classical figures, giving an extremely rich and handsome effect (Plate 79).

It should be mentioned, however, that the Wilsons were not by any means the only potters to produce this type of body and be influenced by the ancient Greeks in their decoration, but a number of their pieces bore the impressed mark WILSON, leaving no room for doubt as to their attribution.

Though the life of the pottery, under various managements, was a long one, it is a

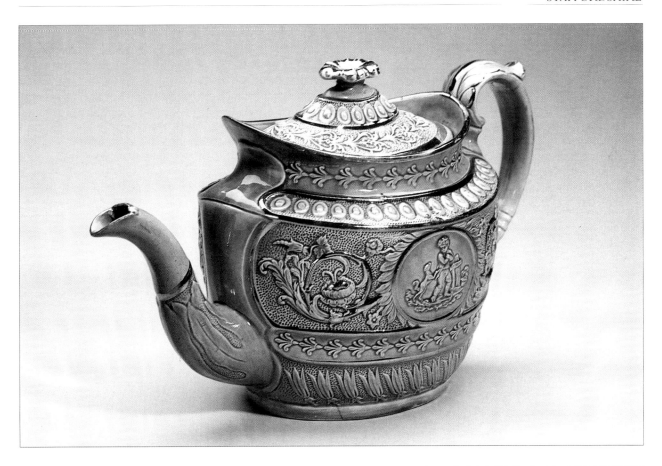

Colour Plate 88. *A highly decorative pale blue teapot, the elaborate and finely executed mouldings highlighted in silver lustre. Probably Staffordshire, 1820s. Ht 7in: 178mm.* (Gutman Collection)

Colour Plate 89. *A moulded 5¼in: 133mm high, yellow-glaze jug, probably Staffordshire c.1820-1825, apparently decorated with raspberries rather than the more traditional strawberries. Alternate leaves are in green enamel and silver lustre.* (Gutman Collection)

Plate 81. *The only surviving photograph of a rather badly damaged but nevertheless important Enoch Wood copper lustre, yellow-panelled jug which was inadvertently disposed of before its significance was realised. The coloured transfer print shown matches similar prints found on broken pottery from the Wood factory excavated in the foundations of St Paul's churchyard, Burslem. These were the remains of finished examples of his work deposited there by Enoch Wood in 1828. The print thus establishes the provenance of this popular type of jug with its distinctive outline and handle shape. It can be found in many decorative guises (see Colour Plate 47).*

failure rate of Staffordshire potters, often through lack of business sense, Enoch Wood, already an established figure in the ceramic trade, went into partnership in 1792 with a local attorney, James Caldwell, so attracting further investments. Under their joint names, at the Fountain Place works in Burslem, they became after 1805 extremely important producers of lustred earthenwares and probably some porcelain as well. Portrait busts and figures were some of the earliest lustred pieces they produced, but they are probably best known for a most attractive range of pear-shaped jugs in a number of sizes with pink or purple lustre trim and decorative sprigging in white or in enamel colours on a very distinctive blue ground. The sprigging often shows vines laden with grapes and other botanical motifs surrounding romping putti or other semi-classical figures. Enough of their jugs and other wares were impressed with the mark WOOD & CALDWELL for us to be able to match their characteristics to other, unmarked pots and be reasonably confident that they came from the same source.

The partnership of Wood and Caldwell came to an end in 1818 when Enoch Wood bought out his partner. He continued in business at the Fountain Works but under the name Enoch Wood & Sons, as he had now been joined by sons Enoch, Joseph and Edward, becoming one of the most important manufacturers of earthenware, lustred and unlustred, in the whole of the Potteries. The quality of their wares was of the highest and a number of their products bore, not surprisingly, a close resemblance to those of Wood & Caldwell. And once again only a number of them bore an impressed mark, this time ENOCH WOOD & SONS. The over-all range was far greater than that of the earlier firm and included jugs in a variety of shapes including a fairly squat design which was to become almost a Wood trade mark, together with bowls, teapots, mugs and so on, a great many of them with copper lustre and wide coloured banding and elaborate sprigging in the gayest of enamel colours. A prime example of this is the jug in Colour Plate 52 with its great white bull on either side and the arms of England, Scotland and Ireland combined on the front. The distinctive enamel decoration round the top is similar to that found on known Wood jugs. There is no mark, but the whole feel and the quality of the piece says in no uncertain terms that it is of Wood origin.

With the style of the copper lustre jug with yellow banding shown in Plate 81 we can be even more certain of a Wood origin. The jug in the photograph was at one time actually in the author's possession without it being recognised for what it was. It was fairly badly damaged and, in a periodic clear-out of what were thought to be less

pity that its time under the Wilsons, when such beautiful and distinctive wares were produced, should have been so short. David Wilson died in 1816 and his son succeeded him in the business.

See also Colour Plate 94 and Plate 107.

Wolfe, Hamilton & Arrowsmith 1800-1810

Thomas Wolfe was a long-established and highly respected potter when, in 1800, he and his partner Robert Hamilton ceased to trade as Thomas Wolfe & Co. and joined forces with William Arrowsmith to form the company that bore all three of their names. Simeon Shaw, in his *History of the Staffordshire Potteries* (1829), claims that a Mr John Gardner, when employed by the late Mr Wolfe of Stoke, was the originator of the process of silver lustring but, though this has since been shown to be very doubtful, it is known that Wolfe was certainly involved early in the lustre story and produced wares of high quality. His name is one that has been put forward as a possible creator of the finely potted group of wares of unknown origin, attributable only at the time of writing to the mythical Factory Z.

Wood & Caldwell and Enoch Wood & Sons 1792-1818 and 1818-1846

Perhaps as a wise precaution, in view of the generally high

Plate 82. *A pair of jugs, both with silver lustre trim and both of Staffordshire origin. The jug on the right, with its drabware body and black transfer print is, according to the latest research reported in* The Northern Ceramic Society's Newsletter, *possibly a product of Factory Z, manufactured some time between 1810 and 1820.*

important pieces, it went to the salerooms. It was not until Dr. Geoffrey Godden saw a picture of it, which had fortunately been retained, that it was revealed that the freely-painted figure of a woman in a panel on one side was exactly the same as one on shards found during investigation of the old Fountain Place site. It would be interesting to know where this jug is now, but its picture has helped in the identification of many other jugs of similar shape but different decoration. In fact, identical decorative motifs have also been found on a bone china teapot, one of several indications that the Wood output was not confined to earthenware. Complete examples of his wares were deposited in 1827 by Wood himself in the foundations of St Paul's Church, Burslem, as examples of the factory's products. These, some still intact, were found when the church was demolished in 1974 and retained by the contractors. Only broken bits ended up in the museum as examples of the work of one of the most durable of the Staffordshire potteries of the nineteenth century, run by one of the giants of the industry.

Enoch Wood & Sons finally closed its doors in 1846, just six years after the death of its founder.

See Colour Plates 47 to 49 and 52 to 55 and Plates 1 and 81.

Factory Z

This rather mysterious designation is used in connection with the manufacture of a distinctive range of porcelains and some equally distinctive earthenware, the true maker of which is not known. They have so many common characteristics that they can with some confidence be placed in one group, but none has been found with marks. Many people consider them New Hall in style and yet other researchers have attributed them to Robert Wilson and to Wolfe's Stoke factory. Much research is still going on and progress is reported regularly in the *Newsletter* of the Northern Ceramic Society. A recent contribution put up the idea that they might come from further north in the Liverpool area, but the truth is still shrouded in a mist through which one can only glimpse a gleam of light.

The name Factory Z, together with two others, Factory X and Factory Y, was devised by David Holgate so that at least the pieces in each category could be classified together under some sort of title.

The present writer is not qualified to throw any new light on the matter, but is concerned with the products attributed to Factory Z, for a great many of them have lustre decoration, predominantly in the form of silver lustre in conjunction with enamel decoration of teawares and used for banding and for highlighting rims of cups, bowls and jugs. Recognising a Factory Z pot and being quite sure of your ground is not easy, but a few pieces are illustrated here (Colour Plates 63 and 64 and Plate 82) which it is hoped will form, if nothing else, a signpost indicating the right direction in which to look.

Colour Plate 90. *Four yellow-glaze children's mugs, probably Staffordshire c.1820. From left to right. a) A mother and daughter transfer printed in black with the wording: 'A Present for my dear Girl', with the single word 'CHILDHOOD' underneath, silver lustre rim. b) Silver lustre rim and* decoration. Ht 2in: 51mm. c) Pink lustre decorated with the admonition 'IDLENESS BRINGS DISGRACE' in an elaborate frame. d) Silver lustre trim and the wording 'A Present for my dear Boy' with the word 'YOUTH' under the picture of the 'Dear Boy' himself.* (Gutman Collection)

Colour Plate 91. *A yellow-glaze mask or satyr jug with silver lustre trim and the masks in enamel colours. There were several manufacturers of this kind of jug and considerable variations in decoration. Some had one mask face only. This one is probably Harley, c.1815. Ht 5in: 127mm.* (Gutman Collection)

Colour Plate 92. *A beautifully decorated pink lustre creamware toast-water jug, complete with lid. Bread, toasted brown and hard, but not burnt, would be put in the jug and boiling water poured over it. There is an integral strainer inside the spout to act as a filter, and the infusion when drunk cold was said to be beneficial for fevers and other ills. It seems likely that specialised jugs of this kind would only be in use with the wealthier families so that great numbers are unlikely to have been made. Unmarked but possibly Davenport. c.1830. Ht 6in: 152mm.*

Colour Plate 93. *One unknown Staffordshire factory produced a range of jugs to this general pattern and with a similar distinctive style of decoration. The scalloped, pink lustre rim was a characteristic of them all. The reverse of this jug features a large basket of flowers, transfer printed with enamel colours, as is the country house scene. c.1820s. Ht 5¾in: 146mm.*

Colour Plate 94. *A very high quality pearlware mask jug with silver lustre trim and banding over a chocolate-brown slip. The white sprigging is of a hunting scene that was a great favourite with many Staffordshire manufacturers, including David Wilson. c.1815. Ht 8¼in: 209mm.* (Gutman Collection)

CHAPTER V

The Potteries of the North-East

In proportion to their size and the comparatively few potteries using lustre in the north-east, the output was formidable, and export was a very important part of it. The two towns with which we are primarily concerned, Sunderland and Newcastle, lie in separate counties, Durham and Northumberland respectively. Sunderland and its environs are at the mouth of the Wear river, much renowned in the nineteenth century as a port and for its ship building. Newcastle lies ten miles to the north-west and has its own river, the Tyne, from the wharfs of which huge quantities of coal were exported. Both Sunderland and Newcastle were in the heart of what was, in the 1800s and in the first half of this century, a very prosperous mining area. It is still possible to see some of the remains of the workings of the hundreds of mines that despoiled the countryside.

The traditions of coal mining and ship building were deeply engrained in the populations of both Sunderland and Newcastle, but there were as well a respectable number of families in which the craft of potmaking was just as much a part of their lives. This had been so for many generations before lustre decoration reached the north-east in the early 1820s, a few years after its development in Staffordshire. It was to become such an important element in the decoration of north-eastern ceramics of all kinds. that, as recounted earlier, Sunderland Ware has become the generic term for lustreware (particularly the pink), from whatever source.

Sunderland

Of the sixteen Sunderland potteries only seven are known to have used lustre decoration, which makes the sheer quantities they produced all the more remarkable. By no means all the output from the Wear valley potteries was lustreware, and certainly in the early days before 1805 it could not have been. The earliest records of local production go back to the seventeenth century and relate to the Newbottle Pottery, which was situated four and a half miles to the south-east of Sunderland town. Silksworth Pottery was also some way out into the country, but otherwise all the Sunderland manufacturers were strung out along or very near to the banks of the river Wear. The North Hylton Pottery and the Low Ford, or Dawson's Pottery, were separated from the rest by being some way up river, but the others were grouped quite close together in the town itself. The Sunderland or 'Garrison' pottery was the only one on the seaward side of the famous Wear iron bridge featured on so much Sunderland ware and was, in fact, quite close to the river mouth. For all of them there was very easy access to the sea, which meant that what developed into a huge export trade could be carried out with considerable ease. At the same time, clays not available locally, such as the prized white clays from Cornwall, Devon and Dorset, needed for the production of creamware, could be easily imported in the coasters returning after having unloaded their cargoes of coal at the London docks, or at one of the ports across the Channel in

Plate 83. *Sunderland ewers were either this shape or hexagonal. This one features two rhymes with floral surrounds as well as a coloured transfer print with a farming theme. There are in addition the typical Sunderland free-hand swirls of pink, mottled lustre around the neck and purple lustre trim. Possibly the 'Garrison' Pottery, c.1820-1830.* (Brighton Museum and Art Gallery)

Holland. Local coal that was not exported was, of course, available to fire the pottery kilns.

The reason for the Newbottle Pottery being situated so far out into the countryside was that it grew up on the strength of local deposits of brown clay suitable for the rather coarse wares it produced. In the same way red clay deposits were to be found much closer to the centre of Sunderland and were drawn on by the potteries lining the Wear river, most of which came into being in the eighteenth century.

The peak period for the Sunderland potters was during the middle years of the nineteenth century, but towards the end a number of factors began to work against them. Prosperity in the mines and the growth in both shipping and the shipbuilding industry, with comparatively high wages paid as a result, created competition which the potteries could not keep up with so that labour moved away from them. In addition, the Sunderland area, with its built-in water transport system, was slow to take advantage of the coming of the more efficient railways, and continued in its rather slow traditional ways. Technical advances in the making of pottery had also taken place on the Continent, which meant that they were producing their own wares to sell at a price which took away completely the price advantage that the Wear companies had always enjoyed. By the end of the nineteenth century very little remained of the once-thriving industry.

In much the same way as Stoke-on-Trent was formed from a number of separate communities, so Sunderland came into being as one town only in 1835, bringing together Bishopwearmouth Panns, Bishopwearmouth, Monkwearmouth Shore and Monkwearmouth, with Southwick not officially joining these four until 1928. So, for the pedantic, the term Sunderland ware used for the lustre produced in the first fifteen years could be said to be incorrect. For the purposes of this book, however, everything from the Wear group of companies at whatever date is regarded as 'Sunderland'.

The coming of lustre did not mean that the Sunderland potters ceased production of the kind of wares they had traditionally produced. These included coarse ware revealing its origin in local clays, services in the ever-popular blue and white, wares with over-glaze enamel decoration and the striking and distinctive transfer-printed yellow-glazed ware trimmed in black They even essayed a limited amount of the so-called 'Gaudy Welsh'.

Shards in the Sunderland Museum collection excavated in 1970-1971 from the site of the old Scott's Pottery spoil heap show various transfer prints used, which include designs under the names 'Autumn', 'Balmoral', 'Fuchsia', 'Hortulan', 'Lambton Castle', 'Rose', 'Scotch Piper' and 'Yew Ting'. Photographs of these in *Sunderland Pottery*

Plate 84. *A two-handled pink lustre chamber pot, probably from the 'Garrison' Pottery, c.1830, showing a sailor and his girl accompanied, above the picture, by the words: 'The Token of Jack's Safe Return to His True Love'. This probably refers to the bun he is holding in his left hand which was traditionally given by a girl as a good luck charm before her sweetheart set sail. Underneath the picture is the short rhyme:*

If you loves I as I loves you
No pair so happy as we two.

show that they differ quite markedly from the very distinctive transfer prints, predominantly in black, used on Sunderland lustreware. The former could perhaps be described as more refined and in the conventional tradition of such decorations, whereas the prints on the lustreware had a boldness and a vigour which the others almost completely lacked.

Pioneered in the 1750s, transfer printing first came to the north-east, according to one account, when brought by Joseph Warburton of the Bow Factory in London on his move to Newcastle in 1757. At any rate William Maling, then of the North Hylton Pottery, was ordering copper plates for transfer printing from the workshops of Ralph Beilby and Thomas Bewick in 1778. It would seem, however, that the transfers only achieved their own, distinctive, north-eastern style in both Newcastle and Sunderland after the arrival of lustre. Many were based on recurring themes involving the sea and sailors, as was to be expected from the produce of an important shipping centre, but there was curiously little reflecting the other great activity associated with the town, that of coal mining. The study of these prints has a continuing interest, for designs so far unrecorded still occasionally come to light. My own researches have uncovered one or two and the Sunderland Museum is always delighted to receive information and, if possible, a picture of any such discovery which can be added to their archives.

The most often recurring theme in the Sunderland lustre transfer designs is the iron bridge over the river Wear. At the time of its construction at the end of the eighteenth century this was the largest single-span cast iron bridge in the world and so the object of more than ordinary local pride. A great many different engravings were used of the bridge at different times and by the different potteries,

Colour Plate 95. *An unmarked Sunderland plaque, with a transfer print hitherto unknown. It would appear to come from a book illustration, an impression strengthened by the fact that it is printed in reverse, the lettering needing a mirror to read it. The notice over the shop door says: MUST BE...OFF THIS WEEK – GREAT REDUCTIONS. c.1820. 8½in: 216mm x 7¾in: 197mm.*

Colour Plate 96. *Richard Cobden, M.P., who fought for so long (and in the end successfully) for free trade and the repeal of the Corn Laws, which finally came about in 1846, is commemorated in this Sunderland pink lustre plaque. Unmarked but probably from the Scott's Southwick Pottery. c.1846. 7½in: 191mm x 6½in: 165mm.*

Colour Plate 97. *A Sunderland wall plaque with a frame of pink and purple lustre, the latter applied to a more elaborate moulding than usual. The warship, combining steam and sail, is THE DUKE OF WELLINGTON – 131 GUNS. c.1820s. Unmarked. 9in: 229mm x 8in: 203mm.*

Colour Plate 98. *A commemorative wall plaque, impressed DIXON Co, and incorporating both mottled pink and copper lustre in the frame. The mock heraldic design has in it the Union Jack and the Tricolor, together with the heads of Napoleon III and Queen Victoria, celebrating the alliance of France and England in 1853 for the prosecution of the Crimean War. The design continued to be used for some years after the hostilities ceased. 8½in: 216mm x 7¾in: 197mm.*

Plates 85 and 86. *Four views, inside and out, of a tobacco jar, probably from the 'Garrison' Pottery, c.1820. Such elaborate decoration would only have been done for a presentation piece, as here for Marshal Richardson. The picture of John Wesley is on the side and under surface of the tamper.*
(Tolson Collection)

some viewing it from one side and some from the other. Some showed the river in comparative calm with only one or two sailing boats on it, while in others it was literally crammed with shipping. Almost without exception these engravings had a brief summary of the main dates and dimensions of the bridge incorporated in the design and occasionally the name of the pottery responsible was given as well. As an example, an actual jug of the 1830-1850 period from almost any of the potteries might have the bridge enclosed in an oval frame round the top of which is the legend (capitalisation of the letters as given) 'A West View of the Cast Iron Bridge over the river Wear built by R. Burdon MP'. Round the bottom half of the print is the following in cursive lettering. 'Span 236 Feet. Height 100 Feet. Begun 24 Sepr. 1793 Open'd August 1796' (Plate 87).

During the main period of lustre decoration the bridge had a gently arched span, but it was rebuilt between 1858 and 1859, this time straight across. Thus any pieces of

Sunderland ware showing the straight bridge, which are less common than the others, must be post 1859. It is worth remembering that the inscription MOORE & CO. Southwick, incorporated into the print described above, is not an absolute guarantee that the jug was made by Moores. Probably it will have been, but the copper plates for transfer printing did sometimes change hands for one reason or another and new owners were often careless about removing another's name from their wares

Usually the bridge transfer prints would have added enamel colours, the latter applied thinly so that the lines of the engravings always showed through, and the whole design would be surrounded by broad, swirling brush strokes of pink lustre, a combination unique to the north-eastern potteries. The reverse side of a Sunderland bridge jug would often bear another transfer print, perhaps of a made-up heraldic design such as The Farmers' Arms adorned with agricultural implements or The Blacksmiths'

Arms, again decorated with the appropriate tools. Sometimes the bridge would be linked to the Masons, with a combination of Masonic symbols, or else to The Oddfellows. Full-rigged ships were enormously popular, a favourite being the 'Northumberland 74', which was the 74-gun vessel that carried Napoleon to exile on Elba. All of these designs would be contained within a frame of some sort, probably of flowers and leaves in bright enamel colours, the whole backed by pink lustre brush strokes. This combination on the white or cream-coloured pottery usually used for Sunderland lustreware was extremely effective. It is perhaps a point worth noting that vine leaves, so much in evidence in Staffordshire pottery decoration, seldom if ever appeared on Sunderland wares.

If the reverse side of a jug did not bear a picture, it would usually be decorated with a transfer of a sentimental, admonitory or humorous rhyme contained within a floral wreath. There were literally hundreds of these verses and it is only a pity that the authors' names were never recorded, for they have entertained and amused collectors (and presumably the original owners of the jugs) over a great many years and certainly deserve recognition. Only a very small proportion were quotations from, or adaptations of, poems by well-known writers. Here are some samples of the others:

Alas how soon this body dies
Its but an earthly clod
Each passing moment loudly cries
Prepare to meet thy God

Let the wealthy and great
Roll in splendor and state,
I envy them not I declare it
I eat my own lamb
My chicken and ham
I shear my own fleece and I wear it.
I have fruits I have flowers
I have lawns I have bowers
The lark is my morning alarmer.
So joly boys now
Here's God speed the plough
Long life and success to the farmer

Let masonry from pole to pole
After sacred laws expand
Far as the mighty waters roll
To wash remotest land
That virtue has not left mankind
Her social maxims prove
For stamped upon the mason's mind
Are unity and love.

The Sailor's Tear
The man doomed to sail
With the blast of the gale;
Through billows atlantic to steer
As he bend o'er the wave

Which may soon be his grave
He remembers his home with a tear.

The Life Boat
Man the lifeboat! Man the lifeboat!
Hearts of oak your succour lend,
See the shattered vessel staggers
Quick, oh quick assistance send
See the ark of refuge launching
See her Hardy crew prepare
For the dangerous work of heroes
Gallant British hearts are there.

A little Health, a little Wealth
A little house with freedom
And at the end, a little Friend
With little cause to need him.

May peace and Plenty
On our nation smile,
& trade and commerce
Bless the British Isle.

My lad is far upon the sea
His absence makes me mourn
The bark that bears him far from me
I hope will safe return
And from his earnings I'll save up
If lucky he should be
And then when old with me shall stop
And go no more to sea.

When first I was a foremast man I often did pretend,
If ere I got promoted I'd be a seaman's friend,
But in a little time I was promoted to be mate,
I then like many others forgot my former state.
When I became a captain I thought myself a king,
I then entirely did forget the foremast man I'd been.

The sun is up we'll brush the dew
And hear the huntsmans gay hulloo
And hark the dogs enlivening cry
Now see the horsemen gallop by
And now we hear the distant horn
Upon the dying echoes borne
From copse to copse the hunters hie
On hearing Drivers well known cry

and finally:

Says Sylvia to a reverend priest
What reason can be given
Since marriage is a holy thing
That there is none in heaven?
There are no women he replied
She quite returned the jest
Women there are, but I'm afraid
They can not find a priest.

Colour Plate 99. *A Sunderland pink lustre wall plaque in the same rare category as the one in Colour Plate 95. The scene depicted in this one is of a courtroom. c.1820-1830, 8½in: 216mm x 7¼in:197mm.* (*Sotheby's*)

perhaps most important of all for the sailors, they were very cheap.

These rhymes were not confined to the conventional Sunderland jugs, but appeared on puzzle jugs, on the large, octagonal ewers with their basins put out by Dixon & Co., on bowls, on teapots, on chamber pots (on which the rhyme would be a distinctly saucy one) and many other items. However, it is with the big, hand-thrown bulbous jugs with their loop handles that they are chiefly associated, probably because one sees more of them at antiques fairs and in antiques shops than almost any other piece of Sunderland ware. The numbers in which they were produced by all the potteries must have been very considerable and they range from those the size of a small cream jug to giants holding 2½ gallons (11.6 litres). These, when full, needed an extra handle under the spout in order to be able to lift them and pour and have probably survived because they were not in everyday use. The quality of decoration on all of them did vary quite considerably but, at their best, they were really very handsome.

The quantity of frog mugs produced by the Sunderland potters was also considerable. Straight-sided and decorated with coloured transfer prints, these contained a surprise for the drinker in the form of a frog (or sometimes a lizard) positioned near the bottom of the inside of the mug, only to be seen when the drinker had all but finished his drink. The frogs were moulded separately and then attached inside the mugs by slip and it is possible, as Deborah Skinner of the Hanley Museum in Stoke has discovered, to place mugs with a particular Sunderland factory based on the moulding of the frogs rather than by any distinguishing factor in the mugs themselves. It is difficult to understand

This small selection reflects the preponderance of seafaring themes. The Sunderland jugs had a special appeal to the sailors calling at the north-eastern ports from European countries and others further afield, and many of them were bought and taken home as souvenirs, as already recounted. They became familiar in many hundreds of homes in the coastal towns of continental Europe for they were immediate in their appeal, attractive as ornaments and,

Colour Plate 100. *An orange lustre bowl with all the usual decorative attributes – a bridge and other prints and a verse and freely-applied lustre swirls surrounding them – proclaiming its Sunderland origin. The interior is as fully decorated as the outside. These bowls were made by a number of*

Wearside factories more usually using pink or purple lustre, the orange in this case suggesting either the Moore or Ball potteries. Dia 8½in: 216mm, ht 4in: 102mm.

Colour Plate 101. *The traditional Sunderland oval-bodied hand-thrown jug, complete with loop handle and a transfer print showing the south-east view of the Wear Iron Bridge, opened in 1779 and built and largely financed by Rowland Burden, M.P. for Co. Durham. Pinkish-purple lustre trim plus decorative swirling brush strokes cover that part of the body not occupied by transfers. The bridge print includes the words DIXON & Co, so that it originated with the 'Garrison' Pottery, c.1813-1819. Ht 6½in: 165mm.*

how watching someone discover that one of these mugs was a joke did not begin to pall, but they were produced in great quantities and over a long period and were not confined to the north-east.

Wall plaques were a speciality of the Sunderland potters though they, like the mugs, were also made elsewhere.

Selling very cheaply, these would take the place of vastly more expensive pictures which the average working man could not afford. Roughly 10in (254mm) wide by 8in (203mm) deep, the surround was a raised, moulded frame decorated in either pink or copper lustre and sometimes in a much less attractive brown enamel. Just inside was usually

Colour Plate 102. *A beautifully decorated pair of jugs, surprisingly of Sunderland origin. An example identical in modelling and decorative style is in Sunderland Museum, attributed to Dawson's Low Ford Pottery. The scene is different on each side of the larger jug, and under the spout it bears the legend 'Wm & Maria Elliot. Married Octr 3, 1843', so it is clearly a marriage jug. The smaller jug has the same scene repeated on either side and only the letters WME in elaborately decorated lettering under the spout. c.1840s. Hts 5½in: 140mm and 4½in: 114mm.*

Plate 87. *A typical coloured transfer print of the Sunderland Iron Bridge, with the name of the pottery, DIXON & Co., incorporated.*

Plate 88. *A very large, 2½ gal: 11.2 litre mottled pink lustre jug. It is likely to be from Sunderland, though the lettering is more formal than usual, probably because this was a specially commissioned example for the Anchor Inn. The front handle under the panel is necessary when pouring from such a large container. c.1840s.*

a band of mottled pink lustre, while the flat centre would contain perhaps a transfer printed religious maxim such as 'Prepare to Meet Thy God' or else something pictorial. This might be a portrait of a religious leader such as John Wesley (Colour Plate 44) or a politician of the day, but sailing ships were also great favourites, as were romanticised landscapes. Some of the later plaques showing early railways scenes are very much sought after today. Inevitably the Sunderland iron bridge was featured on many of them and a fair proportion were marked on the back, usually impressed with the names of either Dixon & Co. or Moore & Co., though these two firms were not the only ones in Sunderland to produce plaques.

The authors of the Sunderland and Newcastle transfer-printed rhymes have remained largely unknown and we are not very much better informed as to the identities of the artists who drew and/or engraved the copper plates from which the pictorial transfers were made. Some of them, especially a selected few of the views of the Wear Iron Bridge, were real works of art and, following on from the pioneer work of Margaret Gill, research is presently being carried out by Nick Dolan of the Tyne and Wear Museum Services to find out who was responsible for them. In the *Journal of the Northern Ceramic Society,* Vol. 9, published in 1992, Dolan reports on his progress. An eagle eye for detail has been needed, but a few of the prints have provided clues in the form of an initial and even more rarely a name, usually tucked away in an inconspicuous corner. The initials 'W.C.' he identifies as probably those of Walter Cockburn, a silversmith and engraver of Bishopwear-mouth, a Sunderland parish, and this would seem to be confirmed by the full name, W. Cockburn, and sometimes just Cockburn, found elsewhere. 'M. Ryles' is another name that has been spotted, and is likely to have been Moses Ryles, who moved from Ferrybridge in Yorkshire to Sunderland and is described in contemporary records as an 'earthenware printer'. Other artists may well have their identities hidden as employees of organisations such as the Bewick Workshops were not allowed to sign their work, but leads are still being followed up with the enthusiasm and persistence so characteristic of researchers in the north-east.

Whether or not much copper lustre was produced in Sunderland is open to debate. In view of the tastes of the time it would be

Plates 89 and 90. *Two very different designs of Sunderland puzzle jugs. The floral design round the neck of the taller jug is a characteristic of the Scott Pottery, and their name is incorporated into the transfer print. Ht 7in:* 178mm. c.1820-1830. (Tom More Collection). *The other jug is rather less elegant in design, and is likely to be from the 'Garrison' Pottery of the same period.* (Brighton Museum and Art Gallery)

incredible that an area so much concerned with producing wares for the popular market would have ignored this very profitable line. Sunderland Museum does contain as part of its collection quite a few samples of copper lustre decorated pottery, but I understand that these represent types almost certainly produced in the Wear Valley and are not positively claimed to be of Sunderland origin. Certainly no marked pieces of copper lustre have been found, and there are doubts, too, about how much silver lustre was made. There seems little doubt that there was some, especially of the type in a brown body moulded in shapes resembling fluted Georgian silver teapots, cream jugs, sucriers and so on. It is thought, too, that Phillips & Co. did produce some over-all silver lustred figurines, but there are no marked pieces in existence as far as is known. Garry Atkins' exhibition *People's Pots* of 1962 showed, and pictured in the catalogue, a Sunderland creamware jug with a coloured transfer print of the Wear Bridge and above it a panel in silver resist lustre containing the words: 'John and Mary King. John King, Branch Pilot No.22, Poole, Dorset, 1815'. The maker was not named.

The typical rounded, hand-thrown Sunderland jugs with their loop handles were for long thought to be the only kind produced in any quantity. Fairly recently, however, as described by Nick Dolan in the *Journal of the Northern Ceramic Society,* Vol. 9, another type of jug has been discovered bearing Sunderland features, of which it is thought there may have been quite a quantity produced. As can be seen from the example shown in Colour Plate 107 with its comparatively big lip and flat-topped handle, these

jugs were much more of a Staffordshire shape, which makes one wonder if many examples may have been mis-attributed in the past. The wide blue banding on the one shown is a feature of the Sunderland product and for the rest there is high quality enamel decoration not at all like that on other Sunderland wares, including a deep pink lustre trim.

Leading on from this, for a long time the author has had in his possession a small, lidless, enamel and lustre-decorated crocus pot of rather bizarre design (illustrated beside the blue-banded jug) which somehow did not seem to fit the style of any of the lustre producing areas. After seeing a picture of the new-style Sunderland jugs, it was realised that a small, circular enamelled motif which formed part of the overall decorative design of the jug was repeated exactly on the crocus pot. Close examination of the brush strokes of both made it virtually certain that they were by the same hand. This appears to place the crocus pot in the Sunderland area (it has no maker's mark), something that has been welcomed by the Sunderland Museum researchers as it fills in one more small corner in their knowledge of the range of artefacts made by the local potters.

Sunderland Lustre gives the recipe for the gold (pink and copper) lustre used during the nineteenth century by the Wearside potters, which it is interesting to compare with the Lakin recipe in Chapter 2. To quote:

5 parts powdered gold with the addition of a little tin were dissolved in 30 parts of hydrochloric acid and 10 parts of nitric acid. This process took about two hours. Separately 30

Colour Plate 103. *A pair of plates of uncertain origin, decorated with floral sprays in enamel colours and with decorative pink lustre borders. The north-east has been suggested as a possible source, and so has Swansea. c.1820s. Dia 8½in: 216mm.*

Colour Plate 104. *A rare toilet tray or dish, easily adaptable as a wall plaque, with a very deep purple and mottled pink lustre border. Inscribed Robert & Sarah Graham, 1848. The rhyme is a Sunderland one. 10in: 254mm x 8¼in: 210mm.*

Plate 91. *An engraving of the new Wear Bridge with a straight rather than an arched span, which replaced the old bridge in 1859. Thus it is to be found only on the wares of the longer-lived Sunderland potteries such as Scott's and Moore's and late-comers on the scene like Ball's Deptford Pottery. This view is from the east and the bottle oven shown on the left is probably that of the Burnside Pottery, not a producer of lustre.*

parts of balsam of sulphur (4 parts crystallised sulphur, 8 parts turpentine and 16 parts linseed oil) and 20 parts of turpentine were mixed and gently heated. To this diluted boiling solution was added the gold solution. By this time the percentage of gold in the solution was only about 3 per cent. The cost of the metal for covering an average pot was less than one penny (0.4p). The gold lustre mixture was applied to the already glazed pot with a fine brush moistened with turpentine. The pot was then re-fired in a muffle kiln. The temperature at firing was comparatively low to ensure that the already applied glaze would not melt. During the firing the sulphur burnt away, thus absorbing oxygen which helped to reduce the gold covering to a metallic state.

One cannot complete a round-up of pottery items (and it was pottery only) produced on Wearside without some description of figurines apart from those mentioned briefly as being in silver lustre. Probably the most famous are those representing the Four Seasons, SPRING, SUMMER, AUTUMN and WINTER, each of a woman bearing fruits of the harvest appropriate to her time of year. These were produced by Dixon, Austin & Co. between 1820 and 1826, the figures themselves in bright over-glaze enamel colours, mounted on mottled lustre bases.

Watch stands or holders were also made in a number of forms and decorative themes, one Dixon design moulded to resemble a miniature grandfather clock. Sometimes this would be flanked by figures of children and sometimes by a pair selected from their much larger Four Seasons quartet. The firm of Dawson is thought to have been responsible for statuettes of many notabilities, including Joan of Arc, the Duke

of Wellington, Napoleon and busts of Queen Victoria, Nelson and Wesley. Very finely modelled bulls in over-all copper lustre are believed to emanate from the same pottery, while others made many of the always popular lion statuettes. In these the lion stands with one of its forepaws on a ball, small scale copies of the marble statues that stood at the entrance to the Loggia dei Lanzi in Florence since about 1775. Other small copies, only quite a small proportion in lustre, had also been produced in quantities in Staffordshire and elsewhere.

The Sunderland cat (Colour Plate 43) was, however, a complete original. Sitting rather stiffly upright, it had the air of an animal deeply offended by a comment that cats look better with fur than they do coated in mottled pink lustre. Pink, or more usually copper lustre was used for the trim of the Sunderland version of fireside or chimneypiece dogs, almost identical to those from Staffordshire. They were in five sizes, from about 6in (152mm) up to 18in (457mm) and were modelled on a cross between a King Charles spaniel and a Maltese lapdog.

Pottery teawares of various kinds formed a part of the Sunderland range, perhaps the most notable amongst which were the plates with pierced and moulded basket-weave edges, the latter usually coloured in green enamel. The centre of each plate carried a freely painted pink lustre design, sometimes of a 'cottage' type country scene or, much more distinctively, strange and exotic, long-necked birds and animals. The latter, from the Sunderland Moore Pottery, appear to have been based on similar plates from the Cambrian Pottery of Swansea. Unless they are marked (as the Cambrian ones frequently were), it can be difficult to tell which are Sunderland and which are Swnsea.

Colour Plates 105 and 106. *A magnificent, rare if not unique, Sunderland bowl, impressed MOORE AND CO. The decoration, both inside and out, is so different from anything else known to come from one of the Wearside potteries that it seems likely that it was made to a special order. It is difficult to date it and there is no inscription that might have helped. At a guess, it is probably post 1850. Dia 11½in: 292mm, ht 6½in.*

Colour Plate 107. *Researchers of the Tyne and Wear Museums Services have in recent years, following the discovery of marked specimens, broadened the conception of what can be considered Sunderland ware to include jugs like this blue-banded pink lustre example. It has what, until recently, has been considered a typical Staffordshire flat-topped handle. Ht 4½in: 108mm, c.1820s. The moulded pink lustre bough or crocus pot, unfortunately lacking a lid, has a small flower motif in the centre near the base, which links it with an almost identical one, possibly even by the same hand, on the jug. If the latter is from Sunderland, so must be the boughpot. c.1820s. Ht 4½in: 114mm, width 7½in: 191mm.*

Colour Plate 108. *A Sunderland mottled pink lustre butter pot of a popular design. It can be seen that the transfer print with the legend: 'Manchester Unity. Independent Order of Odd Fellows', was obviously made for something larger (as was the print of a rhyme on the reverse) as both are here topped and tailed, but it was sensible to get the maximum possible use of prints from expensive copper plates in this way. Floral decoration on the lid suggests Scott's Southwick Pottery, c.1820s. Ht 4in: 102mm.*

Plate 92. *Two north-eastern pink lustre tea bowls and saucers, that on the left bearing the impressed mark of Dawson's Low Ford Pottery, Sunderland, and that on the right a barely legible, ¼in: 8mm-long, impressed mark WOOD.* *This could refer to either John Wood of Hepworth Shore, Gateshead, or Joseph Wood of Felling Shore, also in Gateshead, the latter a town just over the river from Newcastle. c.1820-30.* *(Blakey Collection)*

However, those from Wales are said to have sixty-four perforations round the rim and those from Sunderland eighty-two. Very finely potted and beautifully decorated lustred miniature teasets are more easily placed as they frequently bear the factory mark of Dawson of Sunderland.

Lustre-decorated ceramic carpet bowls round off this account of what was produced in the factories of the Wear. About 3in (76mm) in diameter, they were used in the sport of carpet bowling, very popular in both the north of England and in Scotland in the second half of the nineteenth century. It was played indoors in the long galleries of the big country houses and to stand collisions with the furniture (and each other) the bowls were made of a heavy stone china. This is not a ceramic form one associates with the north-east, where pottery was the rule, so it is possible that the bowls were actually made elsewhere and only decorated in Sunderland. They were more often in enamel colours than in lustre.

THE SUNDERLAND POTTERIES

Dawson's Low Ford Pottery 1799-1864
Founded around 1790 and taken over by John Dawson in 1799, this pottery was at South Hylton (at one time known as Ford), a few miles to the west of Sunderland. It was already a substantial producer of cream-coloured and brown ware when Dawson moved in, but he extended the range and added new buildings and machinery in 1836, thus substantially raising both the quantity and quality of the wares the factory produced. These included transfer printed creamware, and the later white-bodied teaware of

high quality, often with 'cottage' style decoration, plaques, figurines and much else, mostly embellished with either pink or copper lustre. Quite often the wares had factory marks, either impressed or printed. These included DAWSON, J. DAWSON, DAWSON & CO., and FORD POTTERY, SOUTH HYLTON.

William Maling's North Hylton Pottery 1762-1850
Established in the same area as the Low Ford Pottery, but at North rather than South Hylton, this meant this firm was right on the river, thus greatly facilitating shipping. John Phillips, who figures prominently in the story of Sunderland lustreware, was the manager and William Maling's two sons were also involved in the business to some extent. However, it was not until around 1797, when John's son Robert joined the firm, that a major change came about, for he moved the whole operation from North Hylton to Newcastle (taking his Sunderland Bridge copper printing plates with him for continued use, though in a different town), and setting up in what was to be known as the Ouseburn Bridge Pottery.

John Phillips took over at North Hylton but, as he and his family were also very much involved in running their much bigger and more important Sunderland 'Garrison' Pottery, the smaller firm did not prosper as it might have done and met its end as a Sunderland manufacturer c.1850. In its time, however, it produced a range of wares typical of all the potteries on the Wear – lustre decorated and transfer printed creamware jugs, bowls, frog mugs and so on, a speciality being pieces, hand-lettered and ordered by individuals, to commemorate births, marriages and other special occasions.

William Ball's the Deptford Pottery 1857-c.1920s

This pottery was a comparative late-comer on the scene, being established only in 1857. Trained at Dawson's Low Ford Pottery, William Ball came from a family long active in the ceramic industry. His pottery was not particularly close to the river but at this late date easy access to shipping had become of less importance. The coming of the railways, transporting goods much more rapidly than the old sea routes, had to a large extent taken over and Ball was one of those in Sunderland to take full advantage of this, his works being situated right beside the Penshaw branch of the North Eastern Railway. Rail also provided reasonably quick and easy access to the Devon clay he needed and he also used it to import ceramic blanks from Staffordshire for decoration by his own workers.

As will have been gathered, William Ball was a businessman to inspire respect, for his efficiency and enterprise, if not for his ethics. He was one of the most notorious for buying up the copper plates from the bankrupt stock of other firms and using them quite regardless of the fact that they bore the name of the firm from which they had originated rather than his own. He would seem, too, to have been more concerned with quantity than quality and much of the Ball pottery can be picked out for its rather clumsy potting and careless decoration. Quite a proportion of his output was decorated in pale orange (iron) lustre, rather than the more usual pink of the Sunderland factories, and his transfer printing might be in purple, blue, green and brown as well as the more usual black. Ball died in 1884 and his two sons took over, continuing to run the business until well past the turn of the century.

The range of products from William Ball varied little from those of the other Sunderland potteries, but the Jack Crawford rhyme printed on a number of jugs was exclusive to them. It celebrated the exploits of a local hero and ran:

Jack Crawford – The True British Sailor
At Camperdown we fought
And when at worst the fray
Our mizzen near the top, boys
Was fairly shot away.
The foe thought we had struck,
But Jack cried out 'Avast'
And the colours of Old England
He nailed up to the mast.

The line 'Copyright Ball Brothers, Sunderland' appeared under this though there is some doubt as to the validity of its claim. When Ball products were marked on the base in more conventional fashion they used the same copyright notice.

Plate 93. *A very strikingly designed and meticulously lettered presentation pink lustre jug. It bears many of the hallmarks of Sunderland pottery, but shows a refinement in the drawing, as well as in the lettering, and perhaps, too, in the application of the lustre, that is far from typical. Nevertheless, as it also carries a transfer print of the Wear iron bridge, it probably is a specially commissioned Sunderland piece* (Tolson Collection)

Thomas Snowball's High Southwick Pottery 1846-1885

This was another pottery producing lustreware that came fairly late on to the scene but it was never a major force in the industry, employing probably no more than about fifteen workers. The date usually given for its founding by Thomas Snowball is 1850, though there is some question that he may have set up his pottery four years earlier. He produced the usual Sunderland range of wares, but made a speciality of religious plaques, a set of which, presented by the Snowball family, is in the Sunderland Museum. Because of their donor the provenance of these plaques is not in doubt, but no marked pottery from this factory is known.

Thomas Snowball and his brother, Ralph, also ran the Sheepfolds Warehouse in Monkwearmouth, where they specialised in decorating pots, their own and quantities imported as blanks from Staffordshire. Perhaps because of this divided interest of the owners, the High Southwick Pottery did not flourish as it might have done and the end came in 1885.

The Southwick or Scott's Pottery 1788-1896

Situated very close to the Snowball factory in the

Colour Plate 109. *A pink lustre Sunderland wall plaque, expressing a typical sentiment. Unmarked, c.1820. 7½in: 191mm x 8½in: 216mm.*

Colour Plate 110. *An exceptionally fine wall plaque with pink lustre framing a coloured bat print. On the back there is the printed mark of SAMUEL MOORE & Co over the pattern name WAVERLEY, which is contained in a vine wreath and with the word SUNDERLAND beneath it. c.1820. 9in: 228mm x 8in: 203mm.*

Colour Plate 111. *A very handsome pink lustre wall plaque, possibly of Sunderland origin though by no means typical in the treatment of the frame. The country scene depicted is a coloured bat print. c.1830. 9½in: 240mm x 8in: 203mm* (Sotheby's)

Colour Plate 112. *Two out of a set of six Sunderland pink lustre wall plaques featuring coloured transfer prints of hunting scenes. Impressed Moore & Co, they also bear a painted pattern name, the word 'Sporting'. c.1840. 8½in:216mm x 7¼in: 197mm.* (Sotheby's)

Plate 94. *A splashed or mottled pink lustre tea caddy, possibly of Sunderland origin, c.1820. These usually had metal stoppers but one is missing here. Ht 4¾in: 121mm.*
(*Gutman Collection*)

Southwick district of Sunderland, Scott's (founded in 1788) was, after the turn of the century, one of the most important producers of lustreware in the north-east. Apart from having a large domestic market, their wares were much in demand overseas. The company was run by succeeding generations of the Scott family, mostly bearing the Christian name of Anthony, trading as Scott Brothers & Co., Anthony Scott & Co., and Anthony Scott & Sons at various times. They produced transfer-printed wares, both lustred and non-lustred, distinguished sometimes by the transfers being printed on both the outside and the inside of the rims of jugs, mugs and other utensils. The firm's longevity meant that they were one of the few to use transfer prints of the old Wear iron bridge and also, after 1859, of the new one.

However, by the 1870s the firm's fortunes were waning. They found the intense competition both from the Continental factories and from Staffordshire increasingly difficult to cope with and important overseas markets were lost, the decline being helped on its way by falling standards in their product. It was in 1896 that the end came with William Ball, like Lewis Carol's little crocodile, there to 'welcome in the copper plates with gently smiling jaws.'

The Wear or Moore's Pottery 1805-1882

Round about 1805 the old Southwick Union Pottery was taken over by Samuel Moore, with Peter Austin as a partner, though the latter soon departed. The name was changed to the Wear Pottery and under Moore's guiding hand it prospered. His son Charles and nephew both joined him in the business, the former becoming manager. Scott's Southwick Pottery was nearby and it would seem that there may have been some informal agreement of co-operation between the two. At any rate a number of the same transfer designs appeared on both Moore's and Scott's wares.

Eventually the pottery passed out of the control of the Moore family, and the new owners re-equipped it with more modern machinery which resulted in greatly increased production and made the company, by the end of the 1860s, the largest producer of ceramics in Sunderland. After that came an all too familiar pattern of decline and, in 1882, this once so go-ahead business was no more.

In its prosperous days, the Moore Pottery was one of those which quite often used orange (iron) lustre rather than the more usual pink, and they achieved with it some very pleasing effects. Fortunately a number of their pieces were marked, impressed as a rule in a number of combinations of words and abbreviations, all of which included the name Moore. Only on their 'The Bottle' series of plates, which depicted the downward progress of an incurable drunkard, and on their 'California' pattern plaque, did the mark become S.M. & Co.

They produced a wide range of plaques, some of considerable artistic merit. Perhaps the best known, largely because its picture has been reproduced in so many books on ceramics, shows the Sunderland decorator's idea of an eastern palace on the shores of a lake, with a mounted figure in the foreground. The design had the palace on the left and some palm trees on the right, but one can find almost identical plaques impressed Dixon with the two elements the other way round. It is all too easy to confuse the two until one looks at the back.

Apart from plaques, Moore's produced items with pink, purple, copper and probably silver lustre decoration, with bridge views and other traditional transfer print themes. Distinctive, however, was their use on some of them of red, blue and green enamel edging in combination with the lustre. They also put out the range of plates with perforated rims referred to earlier, similar to those from South Wales.

The Sunderland or 'Garrison' Pottery 1753-1865

This pottery, rather on its own and nearest to the sea at the very mouth of the Wear, was next door to the town barracks with its garrison, and it was from this that it gained its popular name, even though the pottery was there before the military moved into the neighbourhood. It was established in 1753, which means that it was very much a going concern long before it turned its attention to lustre in the early 1800s. If there is one Sunderland manufacturer to which items of doubtful origin always seem to be attributed it is the 'Garrison' Pottery, presumably because they were among the most prolific of factories and covered such a wide range of wares, well made and boldly decorated, but with no distinctive family traits.

In a list of known doggerel rhymes used on Wear pottery, which appears in *Sunderland Pottery*, together with the names of the manufacturers that used them, the 'Garrison' Pottery features prominently, though some of the verses were used by others as well. However, if you see the following rhyme on wares from the north-east, you can be reasonably certain it is of 'Garrison' origin.

The Tythe Pig
In a country village lives a vicar
Fond as all are of Tythes and Liquer
To mirth his ears are seldom shut
He'll crack a joke and laugh at smut.

Plates 95a and 95b. *Two views of a pink lustre mug from Maling of Newcastle showing how both the Tyne High Level Bridge and the Wear Iron* Bridge *in Sunderland were used on different sides of the same piece. c.1820.* (Gutman Collection)

But when his tythes he gathers in
True Parson then, no coin no grin
On fish on flesh on birds and beast
Alike lays hold the churlish priest
Hal's wife and sow as Gossips tell
Both at a time in pieces fell
The parson comes the Pig he claims
And the good wife with taunts inflames
But she quite arch bow'd low and smil'd
Kept back the pig and held out the child
The priest look'd gruff the wife look'd big
Z...ds Sir quoth she No Child no Pig.

In 1807 John Phillips, already as we have seen running the North Hylton Pottery, took on the lease of the 'Garrison' Pottery and it is possible the plates for the printing of this rhyme and others came from the smaller firm for, as already mentioned, there was a certain amount of exchange between the two. In 1813, John Phillips was joined by Robert Dixon, whose two sons were later added to the strength. In 1820 John Phillips died and an established potter, William Austin, became a partner with Robert Dixon, carrying on a very successful business until the latter's death in 1844. The number of partners involved accounts for a certain amount of confusion in relation to the company's marks, but the following chronology of the 'Garrison' Pottery from the invaluable *Sunderland Pottery* gives a clear picture. Notice that the true name of the firm was The Sunderland Pottery. 'Garrison' Pottery was never used as a mark.

1807-1812	John Phillips
1813-1819	Phillips & Co and/or Dixon & Co.
1820-1826	Dixon, Austin & Co.
1827-c.1834-1839	Dixon, Austin, Phillips & Co.
c.1834-1839-1865	Dixon, Phillips & Co.

The 'Garrison' Pottery almost certainly produced a large amount of copper lustre (including fireside dogs with copper lustre spots) and was one of those probably using silver lustre as well. For the rest its range might be called, with no lack of respect, the Sunderland mixture as before, except that much 'Garrison' lustred creamware had a vigour about it which made it stand out. There were jugs, mugs, loving cups, watch stands, wall plaques, figures of various sorts including the Sunderland lions and those depicting the four seasons. Not least were the chamber pots incorporating such poetic flights of fancy as:

Keep me clean and use me well
And what I see I will not tell.

SEAHAM

Moving south along the coast, right next door to Sunderland is Seaham, in the 1800s one of many small mining towns and villages in the area. Its harbour was built especially for shipping out coal from the local mines.

Seaham Pottery 1838-1841

The Seaham Pottery at Seaham Harbour, under its proprietor John Allason, was run from 1838 to 1841. Its aim was the production of simple earthenwares and it is only in very recent times that signs have begun to emerge that it was a producer of fair quantities of lustre decorated pottery. If proof were needed, a very large jug willed and now displayed in the Sunderland Museum has the words SEAHAM POTTERY lettered under the spout. It is very much in the Sunderland pattern, full-bodied and with the typical loop handle. Transfer prints and pink lustre swirls again echo Sunderland, though perhaps the enamel decoration has a slightly different range of colours and is more elaborate. It is now believed that a number of jugs previously thought to have come from Wearside actually originated at Seaham. Only rarely were they marked with the name of the pottery or the proprietor, but a possible indicator is that, while retaining the bulbous shape, the lower half tapers fairly markedly towards the base.

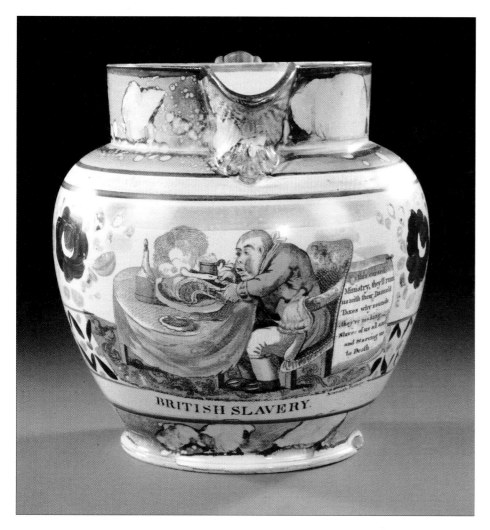

Colour Plate 113. *This mottled pink lustre jug is not, as first glance might indicate, one of those carrying an anti-slavery slogan, but is a protest against taxes which will 'ruin us with their demands and make slaves of us all'. Political cartoons, like this one, taken from a Gillray engraving of 1792, appeared on many 19th century ceramics. In the bottom right-hand corner of the print are the words 'Newcastle Pottery', a mark rarely seen but indicating The Skidderburn Pottery of Addison, Falconer & Co as the makers, c.1810. Ht 8⅝in: 220mm* (Sotheby's)

Colour Plate 114. *An orange lustre Sunderland frog mug, possibly from William Ball, featuring the 19th century Italian patriot GENERAL JOSEPH GARIBALDI, a great favourite with pottery decorators in the United Kingdom. c.1830. Ht 4¼in: 120mm.* (Sotheby's)

Colour Plate 115. *A small pearlware mug from a collection of Sunderland pink lustreware, but the fluted rim and the coloured transfer print featuring GRAND LODGE OF DRUIDS might possibly point more towards a Welsh origin. c.1825. Ht 4in: 100mm.* (Sotheby's)

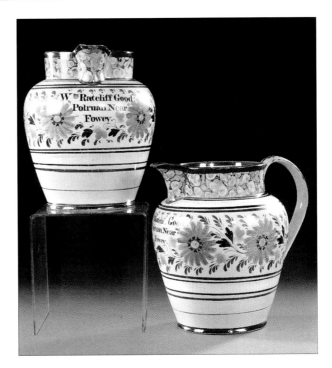

Colour Plate 116. *An unusual Sunderland pink mottled lustre straight-sided bowl (porringer?) decorated with coloured transfer prints on a farming theme, the verse 'The Farmer', and bearing the inscription 'William Goodburn, Febv 23rd 1847'. Dia 8in: 202mm.* (Sotheby's)

Colour Plate 117. *An attractive pair of pink lustre creamware jugs, probably from Sunderland though not completely typical in shape. Possibly they were specially ordered presentation pieces as they bear the inscription 'Wm Ratcliff Good, Polruin, Near Fowey', which is a long way from Sunderland. c.1820. Ht 8½in: 215mm.* (Sotheby's)

Colour Plate 118. *A selection of Sunderland pink lustre frog mugs showing the different forms of frogs from various potteries. The mug top right shows the re-built Sunderland bridge with its straight-topped span, which means it must date from after 1859.* (Sotheby's)

Colour Plate 119. *This rare piece of mottled pink lustre, either Sunderland or Staffordshire is, from its size and shape, an early cigarette box. The satirical transfer print on the lid features a man with a wooden leg in a meat market. c.1880* (Sotheby's)

Newcastle

Newcastle was just ten miles to the north-west from Sunderland and, like it, an important shipbuilding town, port and great exporter of coal. It is in Newcastle that Hadrian's Roman Wall, built to repel the Scots, begins its journey right across the wild and lonely Northumbrian moorlands to Bowness on the Solway Firth on the other side of England. Within the town boundaries, in the district of Wallsend, one can still see some of the surviving stones, though it is necessary to go out into the countryside to see sections of the wall still standing more or less complete after nearly 2,000 years. Up the coast is the spectacular Bamburgh Castle, Holy Isle and Lindisfarne. It is a dramatic area steeped in history, but most of what made it famous industrially in the early 1800s has gone. The mines have closed and the shipyards are idle or nearly so, and most of the pottery manufacturers described here are only names in the municipal records.

However, Newcastle is still thriving, for new industries have taken the place of old, just as they have in Sunderland.

In the nineteenth century no less than twenty-three potteries made Newcastle an important centre of ceramic production. Many clustered along the banks of the Tyne so that they had the same export and import advantages as neighbouring Sunderland on the Wear. Over the years they produced a wide range of pottery, including blue and white and Gaudy Welsh. The firm of Maling was at one time the largest manufacturer in the country of white ware ointment jars and other ceramics for the chemical industry, while yet others produced vast quantities of chimney pots and roof tiles using the local red clay. However, only nine Newcastle potteries are known to have produced lustreware including, later in the nineteenth century, a range from Maling in iridescent lustre.

One cannot help wondering why it should be that, although Newcastle's output of lustreware was probably on a par with that of its nearest neighbour, Sunderland, it is the latter name that first comes to mind when the subject of lustre comes up. The designs of the wares they both produced were, in many cases, practically identical, and Newcastle may even have had a wider range of products that fell outside the standard lines of hand-thrown jugs, frog mugs, plaques, butter pots, ewers, chamber pots, bowls and so on. The answer lies, I suspect, in the Sunderland Bridge prints, which appeared misleadingly on so many Newcastle pieces, though the later Tyne Bridge in Newcastle – and sometimes both bridges together – is featured on some of them. At least one reason for this confusion has already been mentioned, the removal of Robert Maling's business from Sunderland to the Ouseburn Bridge Pottery in Newcastle and the transfer there of his printing plates featuring the bridge. Though causing a certain amount of bafflement for the uninformed collector, there was really

Plate 96. *A very elegant, 11in: 279mm pearlware coffee pot with decoration in pink lustre and predominantly green enamel. Probably Newcastle and possibly from Sewell, though it is unmarked. c.1820s.*

no reason why he should not continue to use them as new plates were expensive items. It would, however, have made it a great deal easier for all if he had not.

Over a period from about 1820 to 1840 there were possibly three other Newcastle factories also making large quantities of Sunderland style lustre jugs, some complete with bridge transfers. Nobody yet knows for certain which factories these were, but their products have been grouped together by researcher Steven Moore under the inclusive heading of The Tyneside School. The background to the first group, which appears to date from 1820 to 1825, is over-all purple lustre, applied with broad overlapping brush strokes, and the colour palette used to decorate the transfer prints is a strong chestnut-red, green and yellow. The green is used to create what appear to be laurel wreaths which surround the cartouches containing the prints, though there is no attempt at actual leaf shapes.

The second group of jugs (see Colour Plate 120), dating from around 1826 to 1830, is much less typically north-eastern in its decorative style and has comparatively little lustre. What there is is confined mainly to rims and spouts, though there may be small areas with a pink lustre wash elsewhere. The thing that immediately catches the eye, however, surrounding a fairly typical range of transfer

Plate 97. *A teapot of a shape popular in the 1800s, pleasingly decorated in pink lustre, applied freehand rather than combining it with a transfer print. It bears the Patterson mark of the Newcastle Sherriff Hill Pottery, c.1840.*

prints, is the repeat pattern of sprays of leaves in brown, a colour that is usually used for the transfer print as well. Around the neck of the jugs, ears of wheat are depicted, once again in the same colour.

Most usually encountered today are examples of the third set of jugs (Colour Plate 122), dating from about 1830 to 1840. They were made in a full range of sizes and, like those from the first group, had darker pink lustre than was usually found on Sunderland wares, bordering on purple, and the enamel colours were generally stronger and brighter, too. The borders round the reserves in which the transfer prints appear were often made up of a bold chestnut-coloured enamel line, from which radiated flecks of green intended, once again, to represent leaves. Bright yellow enamel also usually finds a place in the colouring of the transfer design.

The name of the Low Lights Pottery in North Shields has been mentioned in connection with these jugs, but whether one company was responsible for all three groups seems a little doubtful. In any case, this firm did not commence lustre production in any quantity until John Carr joined them in 1840, which does not fit in with the dates suggested by Steven Moore in an article in *The Northern Ceramic Society's Newsletter* No. 90, of June 1993. The second group in particular is sufficiently different to have come from another source, though there is a link of a sort between it and the third group in that they both shared the use of a Bewick-based engraving of the North Shields lifeboat.

The Low Lights Pottery was a company which, in its early days, from 1814 onwards, specialised in 'brown and black wares of the common kind', and terracotta vases and chimney pots for the building trade. Coming to lustre late,

Plate 98. *A heavily potted, mottled pink lustre cachepot and stand, probably from Newcastle. c.1820s. Ht 5in: 127mm.*

Colour Plate 120. *An example of one of the groups of 'Tyneside School' jugs, so called as the Newcastle pottery or potteries that produced them is or are uncertain, made between 1826 and 1830. With this group, the use of lustre was reduced to a minimum, the rim and spout being virtually the only part thus treated, though there could also be small applications of a pink lustre wash. The main distinguishing feature (they came in a number of sizes) was the brown leaf decoration on the body and the ears of wheat, also in brown, round the top. Ht 7in: 178mm.*

Colour Plate 121. *A delightful small teaset in which the saucer is impressed SEWELL, but this decorative design has been found on wares from other potteries of the north-east, including Scotts and Dixon-Austin, which would seem to indicate an outside decorator.*

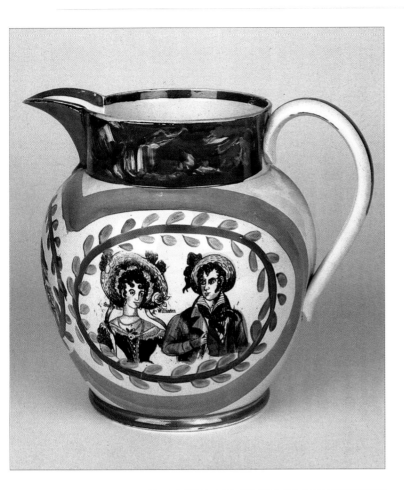

Colour Plates 122, 123 and 124. *Three views of as good an example as it is possible to get of a representative of the 'Tyneside School' of Newcastle jugs, c.1830-1840. It is fully described on page 128 and the original from which the the engraving beneath the spout was taken is shown in Plate 32. Ht 9in: 229mm.*

Plate 99. *A rare plaque framed in mottled pink lustre and impressed C.C. & Co., the mark of Cornfoot, Colville & Co, the forerunners of the Low Lights Pottery, North Shields, when it was run by Nicholas Bird. It had not been realised, until this plaque surfaced, that lustre had been produced by the firm at this early date, c.1829.* (Dr R.K. Henrywood)

they took to it like a duck to water, making a pretty good job of it if they were responsible only for the last of the three groups mentioned above.

One of the most striking examples from group three is the large (9in: 229mm) jug shown on page 127. The main black and white transfer print shows a sailor and his girl, Susan and William, the two chief characters in the melodrama *Black Ey'd Susan or All on the Downs* by Douglas Jerrold, which opened at The Coberg Theatre in London in 1829. This starred Thomas Potter Cooke as William and successfully toured the country, including the north-east, Cooke continuing to play the part, even as an old man in the 1860s. The transfer print on the jug is likely to be based on a toy theatre poster featuring the show. On the front of the jug is another print showing the North Shields lifeboat taken from a poster offering a reward for the apprehension of vandals damaging the lifeboat (Plate 32). This, in turn, was from an engraving by Thomas Bewick. On the reverse side of the jug is the following rhyme:

Here's to the wind that blows
And the ship that goes
And the boy that fears no danger
A ship in full sail
And a fine pleasant gale
And a girl that loves a sailor.

The standard of the lustred wares from Newcastle was generally high. The name of Sewell, for instance, is one that is always associated with work of quality, and the Newcastle firm of Sewell and Donkin of St Anthony's Pottery was responsible for one of the finest pieces of lustreware

illustrated in this book. This is the urn shown in Colour Plate 130, an example of lustre and enamel decoration at its very best. The fine detail of the design is quite breathtaking and the colours that blend in with the vivid jade green of the pedestal have been chosen with the eye of a true artist. Another urn, based on the same pattern, but rather shorter and less elegant, can be seen in Newcastle's Laing Art Gallery, while the Northern Ceramic Society's publication, *St Anthony's Pottery, Joseph Sewells Book of Designs,* edited by Harold and Clarice Blakey, shows that there were several other versions, another of which is shown in Colour Plate 131. All were thrown on the wheel, which would explain some of the variations. Pattern No 46 had a lid, and 46B had a lid and handles. However, it would not seem to have been an item that would be produced in large quantities and certainly there are not many to be seen today.

St Anthony's Pottery also produced a wide range of lustred and other wares including some extremely elegant coffee jugs. They were responsible for the delightful and delicately potted miniature cup and saucer in Colour Plate 121, but not, possibly, for the teabowl that accompanies it. The saucer carries the name SEWELL, impressed, but the teabowl does not. Harold and Clarice Blakey have a marked Dixon Austin saucer which matches and there is reason to think that other firms (including Scott's) copied this most distinctive and appealing decorative design. Either that, or an outside decorator was responsible. Some are reasonably good copies, but I have seen examples of a crudeness that could not possibly have been the work of a quality factory such as Sewell. The very finely-potted canary yellow and silver lustre pot-pourri in Colour Plate 127 is also probably theirs.

The firm of Maling was another notable one in the Newcastle story and grew to a considerable size, with several different factories, making it an important factor in the over-all commercial prosperity of the town. Unlike so many of its fellow potteries, it continued to prosper until well into the twentieth century, finally closing its doors only in 1963. Much the most important period of the firm's existence began, it will be recalled, when Robert Maling moved from Sunderland to open Ouseburn Bridge Pottery on the Tyne. This began production in 1817 so the Maling firm was in existence for something like 150 years, producing an enormous range of ceramics, much of it quite unlike that from any of the other manufacturers from the north-east. It included from the 1920s a wide variety of vases, teawares and so on that were decorated in the sometimes rather gaudy iridescent lustre.

Maling made wall plaques (Colour Plate 126) which were sometimes round rather than oblong and had borders incorporating the green leaves already mentioned in the decoration on Low Lights Pottery jugs. In the 1930s the firm revived some of the traditional nineteenth century lustre designs, but these are quite easily distinguishable as their pink lustre has, for want of a better word, a 'hard' look about it and has lost the mellowness of the original. It is a pity that none of it was marked, for it can easily mislead the modern collector.

Other Newcastle companies that produced many interesting wares were the Sherriff Hill or Tyne Pottery and the St Peter's Pottery of Thomas Fell, together with a number of lesser firms about which information is in some cases rather sketchy. What is known of them and their products, or what is surmised, follows in the brief histories outlined below, together with some additional historical notes on those already described.

THE NEWCASTLE POTTERIES

Albion Pottery 1860-?

This was not an organisation to set the pulses racing as far as its lustre production was concerned. It was very late in the field, only coming into existence under the name Albion when two brothers named Bell took over the old Maling Ouseburn Bridge Pottery in 1860. Later it changed its name to Bell, Galloway and Atkinson when two new partners joined the firm, and the last two names, impressed, were added to the firm's mark.

Lustred wares from this pottery are very rare, but the mottled pink lustre plaque shown in Colour Plate 125 has ALBION POTTERY impressed on the back, the two words arranged round a circle, and with the initial letters of Galloway and Atkinson in the middle. The diameter is 9½in (241mm).

With the same and distinctive broad lustre framing which distinguishes them both from other plaques from the north-east, there is another impressed Albion Pottery plaque illustrated in *Collecting Lustreware*. This one, however, is oblong, 9½in (241mm) x 8½in (215mm), has decorative leaves moulded into each corner, and features a coloured transfer print of a different square-rigged ship. Below this in running script and set in a decorative scroll is a rhyme generally attributed to the Sunderland 'Garrison' Pottery.

In view of the late appearance of the company on the scene, the dates of the two plaques must be given as c.1860.

Collingwood and Beall

This company was another minor player in the league, in that its existence rests on the evidence of one jug only, part of the collection in the Laing Art Gallery in Newcastle. It is fairly typical of Newcastle wares in the style of decoration with pink lustre verging on purple and the use of chestnut red and green leaves surrounding reserves on either side. Both of these carry rhymes, relying on the 'Garrison' Pottery bards for poetic inspiration. The name COLLINGWOOD & BEALL forms part of

Plate 100. *A pink lustre jug bearing the name of Collingwood and Beall under the transfer print of a rhyme, but it is thought likely that this firm acted as decorators for other Newcastle potteries rather than as manufacturers themselves.*

the engraving under one of the rhymes. R.C. Bell, in his *Tyneside Pottery*, locates the firm in the South Shields district, though there are no municipal records of their having been there. However, one way and another they did exist and possibly were a firm of decorators rather than potters.

The Low Lights Pottery 1829-1890

This company, if the idea that it was responsible for the very striking bridge jugs discussed earlier proves to be

Plate 101. *A handsome earthenware teapot, decorated in one of the many variations of the Gaudy Welsh pattern, which usually incorporates a certain amount of copper lustre. Origin uncertain, but possibly Newcastle c.1830.*

Colour Plate 125. *A rare wall plaque with the impressed mark of the Albion Pottery, Newcastle upon Tyne. The broad pink lustre framing appears to be characteristic of Albion plaques as it features on the few others that are known. c.1860s. Dia 9½in: 241mm.*

Colour Plate 126. *Round plaques were less common than the straight-sided ones. This one, 7¼in: 184mm in diameter and with a pink lustre moulded border combined with green flecking, though unmarked, is similar to plaques known to be from Maling of Newcastle. c.1820s.*

Colour Plate 127. *A yellow-glazed pot-pourri, probably from Joseph Sewell of the St Anthony's Pottery in Newcastle. The broad rim is in silver lustre and the print in the oval reserve (repeated on either side) has a silver lustre frame. The print itself is unusual, and not only for Newcastle, as it appears to be based on a Bartolozzi print. Francesco Bartolozzi was a distinguished Italian engraver who settled in England in 1764, where his work had a great vogue, though not generally, as far as is known, as an inspiration for ceramic prints. c.1820s. Ht 5½in: 138mm.*

Colour Plate 128. *A cup, saucer and teapot of an elegant shape very popular with the potteries of the north-east, this set probably originating in Newcastle. Pink lustre in the vermicelli pattern is used boldly.*

Plate 102. *A trio of cream jugs, all likely to have originated in the north-east. The jug on the left is part of a teaset which also includes the sucrier and teapot in Plate 103, plus London-shaped cups and saucers, all probably Sewell,* *c.1830. The centre jug, in silver resist as opposed to the pink lustre and enamels of the others, has matching teabowls, very small at 1½in: 38mm high. The third jug is probably also from the North-East.* (Blakey Collection)

correct, must be counted as having made a major contribution to the ceramics of the Newcastle area. It is a pity, then, that some of its business practices were very definitely on the debit side.

When marked correctly, Low Lights pieces had either an impressed stag's head and anchor, or a printed lion with the initials J.C. & S in flowing script underneath it. Sometimes the words JOHN CARR & SONS, NORTH SHIELDS would be printed in the shape of a horseshoe. However, John Carr, who ran the pottery during the time when it was concentrating on lustre production, was not content with such simple marking. Pattern names in decorative scrolls were also printed on the base of a number of items and these would incorporate such legends as PORCELAIN OPAQUE and WARRANTED STAFFORDSHIRE. Underneath the latter would be placed the initials J.C. & Co, which on the face of it was straightforward enough, except that there was a suspicion that the hope would be that they would be mistaken for those of Joseph Clementson of the Phoenix and Bell works in Hanley. Quite why there was this urge on the part of John Carr for a link with Staffordshire is by no means clear. The Low Lights Pottery had quite a formidable output in its own right and was hardly struggling.

John Carr was not the founder of the company, which was established in North Shields in 1814 by Nicholas Bird to produce 'black and brown wares of the common kinds' and articles such as chimney pots for the building trade. The first indication of lustre being used by the company was discovered comparatively recently when a typically

Newcastle style round plaque turned up. This is decorated with mottled pink lustre with a 'Prepare to Meet Thy God' transfer and has the mark C.C. & Co on the back (Plate 99). It is possible that this was only part of a very limited production under the aegis of Cornfoot, Colville & Co., who took over the Low Lights Pottery from Nicholas Bird, c.1829. Later it became Cornfoot, Patton & Co., and finally Cornfoot, Carr & Patton when John Carr joined the other two. There is little firm evidence of further lustre production until 1856. In that year Carr discontinued the company's traditional lines for the building trade and switched to cream-coloured earthenware, transfer printed and lustre decorated, with which he established profitable trading connections with countries around the Mediterranean and further east on the Indian continent.

A considerable proportion of the Low Lights pottery was decorated in orange (iron) lustre. The typical north-eastern range of bowls, jugs, plaques and so on was produced, and it is difficult at times to distinguish the Low Lights product from that of Sunderland's Ball Brothers, who also used orange lustre more than most of their contemporaries. In general, neither were noted for great refinement in their potting.

Newcastle Pottery 1790-18?

This pottery was not a great producer of lustreware but is known to have put out a range of lustre-decorated jugs featuring engravings of Gillray political cartoons. One is shown in Colour Plate 113 but otherwise the mark appears only on non-lustred wares from Addison, Falconer & Co.

Plate 103. *Elegance personified, the Sewell sucrier and teapot referred to in Plate 102. c.1830. These shapes and small, unhandled teacups, or tea bowls as they are often known, were all typical of the north-eastern factories, which continued to make tea bowls long after they went out of fashion in the south. Not having handles like cups, they had the advantage of being much easier to pack and so were less subject to breakage in transport.*
(Blakey Collection)

Plates 104 and 105. *A pair of cups and saucers from the north-east, one bearing the 'Eel Fishers' print in black with pink lustre trim, while the other is entirely in pink, cottage-style lustre, impressed FELL. (Blakey Collection)*

Colour Plate 129. *A pink lustre moulded jug featuring a stag hunting scene in which the hounds are showing a good deal more animation than the two huntsmen. The figure and the frieze of oak leaves are in enamel colours. The moulded wicker-work of the base is distinctive and is said to indicate Newcastle origin. c.1825. Ht 6in: 152mm.*

Colour Plate 130. *Probably the finest example of lustreware to be illustrated in this book, this handsome vase is impressed SEWELL & DONKIN, so that it comes from Newcastle. Harold and Clarice Blakey's* St Anthony's Pottery, *which includes Joseph Sewell's* Book of Designs, *shows it to be design No. 146, and that there were several versions, one with a lid and one with handles. The decorative scheme could vary, too, as shown by the one in the Laing Art Gallery in Newcastle and also that in Colour Plate 131. c.1825. Ht 10in: 254mm.*

Colour Plate 131. *Another decorative style for the Sewell vase shown in Colour Plate 130. Copper lustre is used for the rim and trimming elsewhere. c.1826. Ht 9¼in: 235mm.* (Gutman Collection)

Colour Plate 132. *An elaborate Sewell (Newcastle) watch holder surmounted by a lion decorated in copper lustre, the latter also used for highlighting such features as the capitals and bases of the columns and the top and bottom mouldings. The multi-coloured finish was of a style sometimes known as marbled lustre and much used by this north-eastern factory. c.1820s. Ht 6¾in: 171mm.* (Gutman Collection)

Plate 106. *A bowl from a bowl and ewer set, decorated with orange (iron) lustre swirls, a Wear Bridge print and the poem 'A Sailor's Tear', surrounded by a floral wreath. A marked piece from John Carr of the Low Lights Pottery, Newcastle. c.1840.*

which owned the Skidderburn works out along the Scotswood Road. Examples can be seen from this pottery in the Willett Collection in the Brighton Museum, but they are not lustred.

The Ouseburn Bridge and Ford Potteries 1817-1963
Mention has already been made about the first of these and how Robert, from the highly regarded Maling family of potters, moved to Newcastle in 1817. The factory had been purpose-built and fired its first kiln on 28 June. Expansion followed and Robert's brother John opened up other premises in 1840, which were known as the Old Ouseburn Pottery. Nevertheless, it was not until the next generation, under Robert's son, Christopher Thompson Maling, that the progress was really consolidated. A chance encounter between Christopher Maling and the Keiller sisters of Dundee, makers of the famous Keiller marmalades and jams, resulted in a very substantial contract to manufacture their jars, a cooperation between the two firms that was to last for many years. Later Malings were to develop this side of the business, making jars for ointment and preserves (in addition to those for jam and marmalade), bowls and basins for the kitchen, butter and jelly moulds and many other domestic items. The export market was also vigorously pursued, particularly in Holland.

In 1859 Christopher Maling completed the building of a completely new factory next door to Ouseburn Bridge. It was equipped with all the latest machinery so that output could be increased once again. This went by the name of Ford Pottery, which became Ford (A) Pottery when it was joined by Ford (B) about a mile distant. Between them the two Ford Potteries made Maling's, despite the fact that they

produced no porcelain, the largest producer of ceramics in the United Kingdom if not the world.

In Stephen Moore and Catherine Ross' book, *Maling, The Trademark of Excellence,* page 26 shows a picture of a small relief-moulded jug in the possession of the present Maling family, with a label bearing the following words: 'This jug was made of clay dug out of the foundations when B Ford Pottery was gitting [*sic*] built. Clay taken to A Ford Pottery, made there, fired and dipt in ordinary glaze.' For a time it was thought that it was a one-off, but since then others in quite a wide variety of sizes have been reported, so obviously the design was put into production, though whether the clay that made them came from the same source is open to question. The jugs are biscuit-coloured with decoration in enamel colours and copper lustre and unlike any other Maling wares.

The company produced an incredibly wide range of high quality designs over the many years it was in existence. This included in the 1920s, as already mentioned briefly, a successful venture into iridescent lustre, using special commercially made lustres. However, with their early Sunderland background, extending over many years, it is not surprising that another side of the business continued with the traditional Sunderland type bridge jugs, bowls, plaques, frog mugs and so on, though a number of their items carried transfer prints of the Tyne Bridge. Some items incorporated both the Tyne and the Wear bridge, one on each side.

Fortunately for us, a good proportion of the Maling output was marked, though these marks varied considerably. One quite frequently seen incorporates a castle and the word MALING. Sometimes the mark is a simple C.T.M. for the Christopher Maling period. A rarer mark from earlier years is ROBERT MALING, which has been seen on a plaque featuring one of a series of favourite Maling prints under the title 'Poor Richard on his Way to Wealth'.

Maling continued production until well into the twentieth century, but by the 1940s it became obvious that the company had not updated its manufacturing techniques in line with the competition, particularly from the continent. As a result, the wide diversity of their products with literally hundreds of designs, something they had always prided themselves on, became less and less practical. Mass-production of a smaller range was tried as an alternative but by 1947 the company was out of the hands of the Maling family and had been taken over by Hoult's Removals Ltd., a firm of furniture removers. One result was that less and less of the Ford B factory was used for the production of pottery but instead for furniture storage. Gradually the removals side of the business began to take precedence and sadly the doors of what had been the most go-ahead, long-lived and successful pottery company in the north-east finally closed in 1963.

Sherriff Hill or Tyne Pottery 1827-1908

From 1827 to 1837 this pottery was run by Thomas Patterson and Co., and a trade directory indicates that some time in the 1850s George Patterson (later joined by a Mr Fordy) was in charge. Whether the two Pattersons were of the same family seems to be in some doubt. The company also moved at least once, being first (under the name Tyne Pottery) at Felling Shore, and later at Sherriff Hill under the name by which it is mainly known. A third address at Three Kings Court, Quayside, is likely to have been that of a warehouse for goods to be exported. A considerable trade was carried on with Norway.

The output was mainly a wide variety of straightforward domestic wares, including children's teasets, many of them with 'cottage' style decoration. Some Gaudy Welsh wares were also in their range. Marks, not infrequently used and all impressed, included PATTERSON & CO., TYNE POTTERY, FORD AND PATTERSON, and SHERRIFF HILL POTTERY, reflecting different periods in the firm's history.

St Anthony's Pottery c.1780-1878

This old-established pottery in the district of St Anthony's was acquired c.1804 by Joseph Sewell, who was joined in due course by a prominent local solicitor and Councillor called Donkin. Under the experienced Sewell's guidance, the partnership prospered and was to produce perhaps the finest and most elegant wares to come from the Newcastle area, though admirers of Maling might dispute this. It could be said, I think, that the Sewell designs, and especially the

Plate 107. *An over-all silver lustre figure of a seated girl reading a book, origin unknown, though possibly Newcastle. David Wilson of Staffordshire was also known for this kind of work. There is a hole in the girl's right hand which could have been for a missing candle-holder. c.1820-30.*

decoration, had a restraint that the sometimes rather gaudy Maling wares lacked.

It was not until about 1815-1820 that St Anthony's started to decorate with lustre, which was, of course, about the time it first came to the north-east. Creamware in imitation of Wedgwood was an early speciality and they were one of the few firms to use wood engravings rather than those on copper plates in their decoration. The work of Thomas Bewick, who had workshops in Newcastle, is featured on a number of their pieces, on which copper, pink and silver lustre were all used in combination with enamels. A damaged saucer, impressed Sewell and Donkin, has been reported by Harold Blakey and is one of only two known marked pieces of Newcastle silver lustre.

The Sewell moulded jugs were often ovoid rather than round and fruiting vines and putti were frequently incorporated in the decoration. Yellow-glazed wares with silver lustre trim and transfer prints in red, quintal flower holders or vases, tea services and decorative wares of many sorts were all part of the Sewell range, perhaps the vase already mentioned and illustrated in Colour Plate 130 being their finest achievement.

Fortunately for us, Sewell and Donkin frequently marked their wares. Impressed marks included SEWELL, SEWELL & DONKIN, SEWELLS & DONKIN and SEWELLS & CO.

St Peter's Pottery 1817-1890

This company was founded by Thomas Fell and Thomas Bell in 1817. White and enamel decorated wares were their principal lines and the output and range of their lustreware was comparatively limited. They did, nevertheless, produce some handsome pieces, including ovoid pink lustre hunting jugs. Early Fell jugs were marked simply with an F. Later marks include FELL & CO, F & CO, T.F. & CO and T.FELL & CO.

Tyne Main Pottery 1833-1851

This company was founded by Richard Davies in 1833 and is included here solely on the strength of a single plate in the collection of Dr. Geoffrey Godden bearing the mark DAVIES & CO, and decorated with a floral design in enamels combined with silver lustre. It seems that the firm did a good deal of business with the Norwegian market.

Wood

This could be either John Wood of Hepworth Shore or Joseph Wood of Felling Shore, both places being districts of Gateshead, just across the Tyne from Newcastle. Mr Harold Blakey has a pink lustre teabowl (Plate 92) and matching saucer bearing the ¼in (8mm) long impressed mark WOOD, which distinguishes it from the marks of Enoch Wood. He points out that teabowls, or more properly 'unhandled cups', continued to be made in the north-east as late as the 1830s. This makes it likely that this one came from that area rather than Staffordshire, and the dates of both the companies mentioned above cover this period. It is uncertain, however, which Wood produced it.

CHAPTER VI

The Potteries of Wales

This group of potteries, the two most important ones being in Swansea and the rest not too far away, was very much out on its own, away from the main ceramic centres. However, despite this isolation and the small number of potteries involved, it was to make a very considerable impact. This was not only for the production of attractively decorated earthenware, but also, at Swansea's Cambrian Pottery and at nearby Nantgarw, for very fine porcelain decorated by many of the leading ceramic artists of the day. They included William Billingsley and Thomas Pardoe.

One might have thought being away from the main stream would lead to completely original styles in design and decoration, as happened to a large extent with the north-eastern potteries. However, as far as lustre decoration was concerned, this was not really the case with Wales.

Much Welsh lustreware was indistinguishable from that of Staffordshire, for which there would seem to be two reasons. In the first place, as we have seen, the leading Staffordshire firms were very much the trend-setters in design and decoration and, if they found successful lines, others were not slow to adopt them as their own. There was no way that Staffordshire could prevent this, and it is clear that the Welsh factories, semi-isolated though they may have been, were by no means unaware of what was going on elsewhere. Also there was a fair amount of movement of workers between the two areas, and Staffordshire designs probably moved with the potters who migrated to South Wales. An example of this was the very handsome pastille burner, or possibly a pot-pourri (Plate 109), which, if it were not impressed with the Cambrian Pottery mark, one would with very little hesitation class as

Colour Plate 133. *Miniature cups and saucers and a plate with broad pink lustre banding, the saucers and plate with 'The Cottage Girl' transfer print in* *puce. The cups have another pastoral scene in the same colour. Probably the Glamorgan Pottery. c.1820. Plate dia 4in: 102mm, saucer dia 4¼in: 108mm.*

Colour Plate 134. *Though these jugs are unmarked, the upright style and 'cocked up' handle indicate a Swansea origin, probably the Cambrian Pottery. Making use of pink lustre and red and green enamel, the strawberry vine* *decoration was a favourite with the Welsh factories. c.1820s. Ht to top of handles 6in: 152mm.*

Wedgwood. Virtually identical pieces came from the Staffordshire factory, though in black basalt rather than silver lustre combined with a deep, luminous, underglaze blue.

Quite how soon lustre decorating reached Wales after its introduction in Staffordshire in 1805 is not known for certain, but it would seem likely that it travelled south perhaps a little faster than it did to Sunderland and Newcastle in the north-east. Sale catalogues of the Cambrian Pottery for 1808 already included lustre-decorated wares.

Despite this, there is no consensus of opinion on how much lustre of any kind was produced over the years that followed by the Welsh potteries, but the catalogues, together with invoices from the Cambrian Pottery's London Showroom, plus the number of marked pieces still to be found today, combine to show that the output of Welsh lustreware, both silver (including resist) and pink, was far from negligible. The use of 'cottage-style' decoration in pink lustre was popular in Wales as it was further north.

As far as copper lustre was concerned, it seems likely that there was far less produced than is commonly supposed, though it is difficult to be dogmatic about this. Even the clays from which it was made appear to be indistinguishable from those from other areas, making it doubly difficult to be sure. True both John and Baker's *English Lustre Pottery* and Morton Nance's *The Pottery and*

Plate 108. *The decoration on this sporting jug is silver resist on sepia. Its origin could be either Swansea or Staffordshire, c.1820.*

Plate 109. *The lid is missing from this handsome piece, making it uncertain if it is a pastille burner or a pot-pourri. Impressed SWANSEA, it has an almost exact counterpart in the Wedgwood range. The bowl is silver lustre, the dolphins a rich, deep, underglaze blue, and the base black. c.1830. Ht 5½in: 140mm.*

Porcelain of Swansea and Nantgarw show a good many unmarked copper lustred jugs with squat, rounded bodies that they attribute to Wales, but it seems likely that this attribution, with a fair proportion of them, must be based on the the say-so of Welsh people in whose families they have been handed down over several generations. Other pieces they show may equally well be of Staffordshire origin.

There are fairly substantial collections of likely Welsh lustrewares, a number of them marked, in the National Museum of Wales in Cardiff, the Glynn Vivian collection in Swansea, and the Welsh Folk Museum, lying geographically between the two.

The Cambrian Pottery 1783-1869

The most important Welsh manufacturer was the Cambrian Pottery in Swansea. In 1783 the site of what had originally been a copper works but was now a pottery, situated between the River Tawe and the Swansea Canal, was advertised as follows:

A very capital Set of Works, well calculated for the Pottery, Glass or any other business, wherein well constructed cones are necessary…There are two excellent Water Mills included in the premises for the grinding of flints… Teignmouth Clay is to be delivered at the works at 12s. per ton, and Flints for 20s.

The lease was taken up by a Mr George Haynes, who enlarged the property as the firm prospered under his direction, and who was responsible for calling the new

business the Cambrian Pottery. In 1790 he entered into a partnership with the Coles family who owned the lease, but it was still Haynes who was the driving force. When John Coles died in 1800, Haynes continued to run the factory on his own, producing a wide range of earthenwares.

In 1802 there was a change that was to have a dramatic effect on the fortunes of a company which, already successful, had yet to reach pre-eminence. It was in that year that Haynes sold the property to William Dillwyn, a business man of Welsh descent though born in the United States, who bought it, not for himself, but for his son, Lewis Weston Dillwyn, who was then just twenty-four years of age and had no experience whatever of the pottery industry. Although he had ceased to be the owner, George Haynes stayed on as a partner, the company now being known as Haynes, Dillwyn & Co. The two appear to have worked well together for a while, but relationships after ten years or so became strained. Robert Pugh, in his *Welsh Pottery*, goes into the matter very fully and speculates that the problem was probably the difference in age and experience. Dillwyn, the younger man and without Haynes' background in the pottery industry, was the senior partner with seven-tenths as opposed to three-tenths interest in the business, and perhaps this was asking for trouble. The retirement of Haynes in 1811 brought the association to a rather acrimonious close.

An early trade card advertised at the Cambrian warehouse in London the 'New Golden Lustre' and, in the same year, a whole range of other lustred items was auctioned on behalf of the firm at Christie's, then in Pall Mall. But the list of goods for sale does leave a question mark. Nowhere does it say specifically that all the lots were of Cambrian manufacture, and in all probability the Dillwyn warehouse also stored and distributed goods produced by others. Descriptions in the catalogue included 'many Services of Table, Dessert and Breakfast porcelain' but, at that early date, the output of the Cambrian Pottery was almost certainly confined to earthenware, of which there was a preponderance in the sale.

Even better as evidence of what the Cambrian Pottery produced was contained in the catalogues of three other sales of warehouse stock carried out when the London premises were given up in 1808. Sometimes the lists were headed 'Lustred Wares' and sometimes lustred items were interspersed with items decorated in other ways. A sale on 21 April 1808 included:

Lot	4	Eight lustre eggs
	10	Six jugs painted and lustre
	65	Three lustre essence vases and covers
	85	Five flower vases, lustre and painted border
	86	An urn with handles, lustre and painted & a pair of beautiful vases and covers
	111	Pair of lamps and candlestick

For other sales the lots included a wide variety of jugs, lustred vases on a yellow ground, hyacinth pots, goblets, a broth basin, mugs, sandwich sets with trays, match pots, flower vases and a set of sphinxes. It can be assumed that, as early as 1808, the decoration would be with silver lustre only.

'Sandwich Sets' may, perhaps, need a little explanation. They were very popular in their day and were made up of covered dishes, shaped as segments of a circle, so that they fitted into a round mahogany tray which had a covered bowl in the centre. Examples are illustrated in Morton Nance's book, though the ones he shows are not lustred.

The main problem with these sales catalogues is that they were not illustrated and we cannot always match the descriptions to wares we know, or are pretty certain, came from the Cambrian Pottery. However, one description does match reasonably well that of 'Three beautiful lustre jugs, painted with roses' and there are examples of these in Colour Plates 135 and 136 of this book, illustrating clearly the flowing strokes with which they were executed.

Lewis Dillwyn may not have been an experienced potter, but he was a man of taste whose expertise in his early career had been in natural history. He was joint author of books on the subject and his passion for the countryside was reflected in the decoration of many of the Cambrian wares. W.W.Young, who at one time had carried out illustrations for Dillwyn's published works, was employed by the firm to decorate creamware and later porcelain with the birds, butterflies and sea-shells in which he specialised. In due course some of the most highly skilled decorators in the country were to join the team, while Thomas Pardoe had been a leading Cambrian artist-decorator since before Dillwyn's time.

In 1814 that nomad of the ceramic world, William Billingsley, pitched his tent at the Cambrian Pottery for a while. He had been for one brief year at Nantgarw, nearer to Cardiff than Swansea, where he and his partner, Samuel Walker, had set up the Nantgarw China Works to produce and decorate the finest porcelain. Through problems in manufacture the venture was not entirely successful and the pair came to Swansea, where their joint experience was put to good use in improving even further

Plate 110. *Part of the Keiller cow-creamer collection in the Potteries Museum, Hanley. The creamer on the left is from a Staffordshire pottery, and the other two, combining green enamel bases with mottled pink lustre, probably from the Glamorgan Pottery, though the one on the far right, judging by its vacant expression, might find it difficult to remember where it came from!*
(Potteries Museum, Hanley, Stoke-on-Trent)

the quality of Cambrian wares, especially the porcelains. However, they returned to Nantgarw in 1816.

Silver lustre at the Cambrian Pottery is usually represented by a range of medium-sized, unmarked, but very distinctive transfer printed jugs in blue with a silver lustre background. The prints are generally of hare coursing or show sportsmen out snipe shooting with dogs and enormously long guns, and are usually considered to be of

Plate 111. *The purple lustre and chestnut red spotting on this cow-creamer or cream jug indicate a Cambrian Pottery origin. c.1825. Ht 4in: 102mm.*

Colour Plate 135. *A Swansea jug of more conventional shape than the sample shown in Colour Plate 136, but with the same style of decoration. c.1820. Ht 5½in: 140mm.*

Colour Plate 136. *A jug with typical Welsh rose decoration, either from the Cambrian Pottery or possibly the South Wales Pottery at Llanelli, painted in bold, free strokes of pink lustre on a paler pink lustre wash ground. c.1820. Ht 6½in: 165mm.*

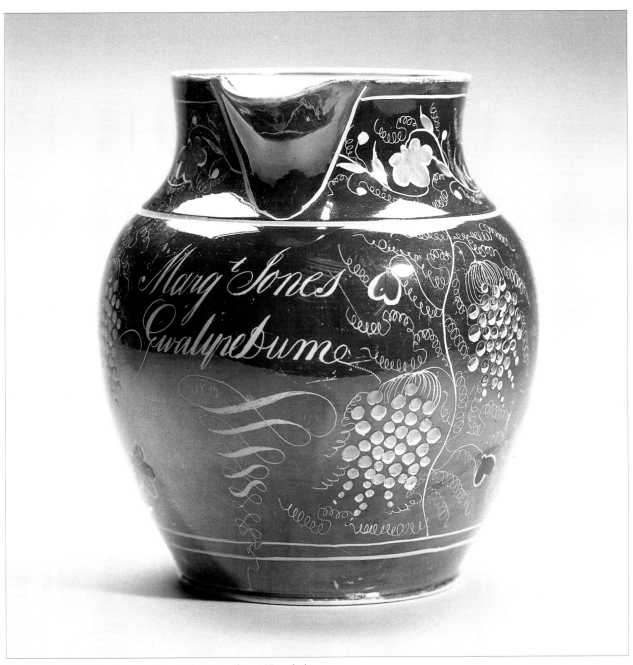

Colour Plate 137. *A handsome purple resist lustre jug, 7¾in: 197mm high and probably Swansea, inscribed 'Mary Jones Gwalyredume, 1813'.*
(Gutman Collection)

Haynes/Dillwyn origin. Also in the Cambrian range were reversible flower and candle holders known as cassolettes with the same blue and silver lustre decoration and incorporating silver resist lustre bands of fruiting vines round their tops. It is, however, when we come to pink lustre that we find most of the pieces which we can be sure about and it is not too rare to find them impressed with various combinations of the words DILLWYN, HAYNES, and CAMBRIAN POTTERY, or just the single word SWANSEA.

The so-called 'Gaudy Welsh' designs, most of which incorporated a small amount of lustre, might be expected to feature in the output of any of the Welsh potteries and the Swansea Museum does have representative pieces in its collection. They are, however, unmarked and similar examples can also be found in the museums of the north-east, Staffordshire and elsewhere, listed just as confidently as local products. The truth is that nobody knows just where this particular type of pottery decoration originated, but it seems that it acquired its name in America, where it was thought for some unexplained reason to be Welsh. No 'Gaudy Welsh' can be laid definitely at the Cambrian Pottery's door, but the museum does have examples of octagonal, rather similarly decorated moulded jugs which they attribute to Dillwyn. They have some lustre decoration and the wording CYMRO STONE CHINA moulded into their bases. Morton Nance gives the constituents as flint, china-stone, china-clay, and ball-clay which, with quite a high firing temperature, produced a result not quite as hard as Mason's ironstone, but at least half-way there and very durable.

In later years Lewis Dillwyn lost some of his enthusiasm and leased the premises to others for a while. This was a period of mixed fortunes with a number of people coming and going in positions of responsibility, though it does not seem that production was seriously affected. Then, seven years after he gave up active participation in the running of the business, Dillwyn's interest was rekindled and he once more assumed command, at the same time purchasing the rival, though much smaller, Glamorgan Pottery.

Cambrian Pottery marks were generally one of the following, though there were other variations:

c.1783-1810
CAMBRIAN POTTERY, painted or impressed
c.1820 onwards
DILLWYN & COMPANY or
HAYNES, DILLWYN & CO
CAMBRIAN POTTERY
    SWANSEA

Sometimes the Dillwyn and Haynes names were impressed in the form of a horseshoe and, as mentioned earlier, the word SWANSEA was also used on its own.

The Glamorgan Pottery 1816-1838

This concern came to be linked really quite inadvertently, and not always too happily, with the Cambrian Pottery, the two being situated close together, sandwiched between the River Tawe and the Swansea Canal. William Baker, Glamorgan's founder, was the son-in-law of George Haynes of the rival establishment and Lewis Dillwyn was not too happy about the connection. There does not seem to have been any impropriety resulting from the relationship, but just the same it was not an ideal situation as, in the early days at least, there was a marked similarity between the products of both potteries. If one produced a new design, the other was quick to follow and the Cambrian lustre plates with perforated rims were copied so meticulously by Glamorgan as to be virtually indistinguishable. So, too, were many of the jug designs from both firms.

The Glamorgan Pottery was built in 1816 so that it was very much a newcomer in relation to the Cambrian. William Baker was joined in the enterprise by four partners, Robert, Martin and William Bevan and by Thomas Irwin, who was William Bevan's brother-in-law. Baker could hardly have picked a better team for, very unusually in what is

generally regarded as a somewhat precarious industry, the partnership remained unchanged until the company finally ceased production towards the end of 1838.

As we have seen, Lewis Dillwyn took over the property, but it was not used as a pottery again.

The South Wales Pottery 1839-1859

This was situated in the town that we now call Llanelli some ten miles or so east of Swansea, though at the time of the South Wales Pottery it was spelt Llanelly. The pottery was founded by William Chambers in the same year that brought the demise of the Glamorgan Pottery. He came from a family that had for long been one of the largest landowners in the district, taking an active interest in the affairs of the town, and he saw that the replacement of the other pottery by one in Llanelly would benefit both himself and the community in which he lived.

There is a marked similarity between the early designs that came from the South Wales Pottery and those that had been produced by the now extinct Glamorgan Pottery and it has long been assumed that William Chambers bought and used their moulds and printing plates. However, according to Robert Pugh, joint author of *Llanelly Pottery*, this was not so. He points out that it would be most unlikely that Lewis Dillwyn, who took over the vacated Glamorgan premises and presumably their contents, would have let the moulds and copper plates out of his sight. He had just seen off one rival company and would be unlikely to encourage a successor. The similarity of the output of the two factories must therefore be put down to the then universal habit of using the inspiration of another to one's own advantage. The presence in Llanelly of William Bryant,

Plate 112. *Wales was the producer of some supremely beautiful wares and some not so beautiful. The drabware milkjug, said to be from the Glamorgan Pottery, must come into the latter category. It has pink lustre trim and enamel decoration on the sprigging. c.1820.*

Plate 113. *Three Swansea pink lustre plates showing a perhaps even odder range of animals than those featured in the Leeds 'zoo'. c.1820s. Dia 8in: 203mm.* (Sotheby's)

late of both the Cambrian and the Glamorgan potteries, as clerk and agent respectively, may also have had something to do with it.

William Chambers continued in control for some sixteen years until 1855, when his father died. Family problems resulted in his deciding to leave Llanelly, though he did retain the lease of the property.

Evidence of a wide range of lustreware coming from the South Wales Pottery does not really exist. There are, however, in the Parc Howard Art Gallery and Museum in present day Llanelli, two over-all copper lustre jugs with views of Neath Abbey on one side, together with a transfer printed clock face incorporating the signature 'Wm Chambers Jn.' as part of the print. The lustre is not particularly well done, reflecting, perhaps, lack of familiarity with the medium. Similar clock jugs are not really rare, but it is agreed that only those bearing the William Chambers signature can be firmly attributed to Llanelly. Otherwise just a few rare pieces of lustre are marked either CHAMBERS LLANELLY or, for the period 1839-1859, the initials S.W.P. printed or impressed.

Welsh Cowcreamers

Based originally on silver models from the previous century, these consisted of small, hollow pottery cows standing squarely on four feet on a moulded base, heads erect, with their tails looped over their backs to form handles and a small lid in the middle of their backs covering the opening through which they were filled. The

milk or cream came out of their mouths and they must have been great places for the breeding of bacteria, for it would be almost impossible to clean the insides. Nevertheless, they were extremely popular and were made in a number of centres apart from Swansea.

The Yorkshire cows are fairly distinct, but those from Staffordshire and those from Wales can easily be confused, for they are very similar (Plate 110). However, comparison of the bases on which the cows were mounted provides a guide. Those from Staffordshire formed quite smooth, formal rectangles while the Welsh bases had rounded ends and were both moulded and painted green to resemble grass.

Cowcreamers from Dillwyn were not all lustred, but those that were usually had pink or purple lustre patches on their sides, making a striking contrast to the white body. A number had black transfer prints of flower garlands on their sides.

The cowcreamers from the Glamorgan Pottery were probably more varied in their decoration, though the actual modelling of the cows varied little from that of Dillwyn. Some featured black transfer prints of landscapes along their sides (not to be confused with the floral decoration on some from the Cambrian Pottery), and the cows' horns, hooves, ears and mouths would be in black enamel as opposed to the pink/purple lustre used by the Cambrian decorators (Plate 111). Others from Glamorgan would be completely covered in pinkish-purple mottled lustre.

CHAPTER VII

Lustreware in Yorkshire

The reputation for very high quality lustreware that is associated with Yorkshire is carried almost entirely on the shoulders of one factory. And broad shoulders they are, for they belong to the Leeds factory of Hartley, Greens & Co., producers not just of lustre decorated wares but of a wide range of other earthenware unsurpassed by any of their rivals. These were decorated in many ways, but quite often the creamware body, perhaps of intricate basketwork, would be sufficiently ornamental in itself and needed no decoration. A simple, colourless glaze over the cream body was enough.

There were, of course, a number of other fine Yorkshire potteries, among them Castleford, the Don Pottery, Ferrybridge, the Swinton Pottery and, of course, the Stafford and the Middlesbrough Potteries rather out on their own near the coast. The last two were sizeable producers of lustred wares, though not on a par with Leeds when it came to quality, but evidence of lustre coming from the other four is very scanty.

Castleford Pottery 1803-c.1870
Daniel Rich, writing in 1922 in the American magazine

Antiques, gave a very detailed description of Castleford lustred jugs, an article that was to be reprinted in 1980 in the book *English Pottery and Porcelain,* edited by Paul Atterbury. This, unfortunately, does not contain a single illustration of the lustreware described, and it seems likely that Daniel Rich mistakenly based his attribution on moulded earthenwares that had motifs similar to those on Castleford-type stonewares. No further reports of Castleford lustreware have been forthcoming since Rich's article.

The Don Pottery 1790-c.1880
'In toilet services many excellent patterns are produced, both enamelled, gilt and lustred, as are the dinner, tea, dessert and other services, and all the usual variety of goods for home and foreign consumption.' Jewitt is referring, however, to a period quite late in the nineteenth century and we have no knowledge of lustreware being produced by this important factory during its early period. It would be strange, however, if there were none, for the company had links of a sort with Leeds, who were leaders in this field.

Plates 114 and 115. *A silver resist on creamware jug with the unmistakable Leeds lion, straight out of The Wizard of Oz, on one side and a typical rather spiky-feathered bird on the other. c.1815. Ht 6½in: 152mm.*

(Gutman Collection)

146

Situated at the most southerly of the three Swintons in the south Yorkshire coalfield not all that far from Doncaster, this pottery was on the banks of a canal which linked it directly with the River Don (from which it got its name) and eventually with the Humber and the port of Kingston upon Hull on the North Sea coast. It began production during the last ten years of the eighteenth century but then, in 1800, took great strides forward under the management of John Green of the same family as the proprietors of the Leeds factory. John Green's two sons were to join him in 1807, the company going then under the name Greens, Clarke & Co. William Clarke was a rope manufacturer who also came in as a partner and John and William Brameld from the old Swinton Pottery joined the venture at the same time. It was a successful partnership and continued to prosper after the death of John Green quite early on. In fact it lasted for nearly thirty years, the firm becoming the largest producer of ceramics of all the Yorkshire potteries. However, in 1834, financial problems forced the sale of the company to Samuel Barker of the Old Pottery at Mexbrough, who continued to run it as a profitable exercise for many years under his stewardship.

The links with the Leeds Pottery that came about through members of the Green family being involved in both companies showed most notably in the pattern books, that of the Don Pottery containing many engravings which

Plate 116. *A fine silver resist lustre bowl, probably from Leeds c.1820, 12¼in: 310mm in diameter and 5in: 127mm deep.* (Gutman Collection)

were identical to those in the Leeds. There were actually more designs in the Don book, 292 as against 269, but there could be little doubt that many engravings in both books had actually come from the same source. It appears almost as if one had been traced from the other and, if so, one would presume that this was done by agreement. Copying a rival's design was common enough as we have

Plate 117. *Though none of these three silver resist jugs is marked, the pattern of small leaves on the centre and left-hand jugs is attributed in* English Lustre Pottery *to the Leeds factory, but confirmation is lacking. c.1820-1825. Hts 5in: 127mm, 6½in: 165mm and 6in: 152mm.*

Plate 118. *Though unmarked, this loving cup is decorated in silver resist lustre very much in the Leeds style. c.1820. Ht 5½in: 140mm.*

Plate 119. *A very large, (7¾in: 197mm) jug with typical Leeds silver resist decoration, the body in very light, creamy-white earthenware. c.1820s.*

seen, but to produce what almost amounted to a facsimile of another's pattern book would hardly have been acceptable.

The Don pattern book covered a vast range of wares, including every conceivable type of tableware, and so great was the output that at one time no less than eight kilns were needed for the firing. Paintings of flowers were frequently used in the decoration and also lustre. But we do not know for how long a period lustring was carried out and to what extent. The fact that no marked Don lustre-ware is known might indicate that there was not very much, but marking of any of the Don wares was the exception rather than the rule. Where marks do occur, they are likely to be:

DON POTTERY

or   GREEN
DON POTTERY

Even more rare are the words Don Pottery in red enamel.

Ferrybridge Pottery 1804-1834

This pottery was situated only a few miles east of Castleford on the banks of the River Aire, not far from where it joined the Aire and Calder Navigation, linking it, like the Don Pottery, directly to the Humber and Kingston upon Hull. It was founded in 1793 by William Tomlinson and a number of partners and, first known as the Knottingley Pottery, traded as Tomlinson, Foster & Co.

When Ralph Wedgwood joined them in 1798 this appeared to be a considerable coup and his name was added to that of the other two partners in the company title. Ralph was the son of Thomas Wedgwood of Etruria who was a cousin and partner of Josiah Wedgwood, and for a time had carried on business on his own account as Wedgwood & Co. However, he was far from being the ideal partner at Ferrybridge, for he was far too prone to making impractical experiments which only produced wares much subject to breakage, which were a waste of time and materials. The new partnership did not last beyond 1800, but William Tomlinson continued to trade on his own, in 1804 changing the company's name from the Knottingley Pottery to the Ferrybridge Pottery. By 1805 he had been joined by yet another partner, John Plowes, late of the Castleford Pottery. The company continued in production until 1834, by which time Tomlinson, well into his eighties, was sole proprietor.

Plate 120. (Left) *A Sunderland watch stand impressed DIXON AUSTIN and dating from c.1825. 11in: 279mm high. The stand, in the form of a long-case clock with the main body decorated in mottled pink lustre, is flanked by two children. Other versions had two adult figures, selected from the Dixon Austin 'Four Seasons' set. Pink lustre trim was supplemented by enamel* colours. (Right) *A fine silver resist bough pot. Though unmarked, the very typical Leeds bird decoration, together with the fine quality of the resist work, are indications of its possible Yorkshire origin. A very similar one, attributed to Leeds, is pictured in John and Baker's* Old English Lustre Pottery.

(Russell, Baldwin & Bright)

Ferrybridge produced a wide range of wares and had a considerable export business, with Russia as one of its major customers. Jewitt describes a brief flirtation the factory had with the production of china, though this did not continue. During Ralph Wedgwood's time, Jewitt recounts: 'Cameos, medallions and other ornamental articles were made in imitation of those of Josiah Wedgwood, to which they were, however, very inferior both in body and finish.' They were, it might be added, often impressed WEDGWOOD & CO, which was highly confusing. A scrapbook relating to the work of Ralph Wedgwood entitled *Wedgwood & Co. Ferrybridge Shape and Pattern Book* is in the Wedgwood Museum at Barlaston and gives a broad picture of the range of Ferrybridge wares and their decoration, but it would seem that much of the content belongs to Ralph's Burslem period rather than to Yorkshire. Just how much lustre decoration was done is not known, but as by no means all Ferrybridge wares were marked there may well be more of it than is realised. A visit to The Castleford Library Museum Room provides firm

evidence that there was some. Pieces with the impressed mark FERRYBRIDGE/B include a plate decorated with pink lustre houses and trees, and a cup and saucer with pink lustre oak leaves. Like many Ferrybridge wares, they are not of particularly high quality.

Leeds Pottery 1783-1828
This was established in the parish of Hunslett on the south side of Leeds by Joshua Green round about 1770, and there were two main reasons for choosing its location. First it was on the freight line linking it directly with a coal supply for the bottle ovens from the Middleton Collieries and second it was not very far distant from the natural clay deposits of the Wortley Hundreds to the west. Of these, Ralph Thoresby in his work *Ducatus Leoniensis* published in 1714 wrote: 'Here is a good vein of fine clay that will retain its whiteness after it is burnt (when others turn red) and therefore used for making tobacco pipes, a manufacture but lately begun in Leeds'. Leeds clays were renowned for lightness of weight, which was reflected in the weight of

Plate 121. *Apart from its prime function of puzzling the would-be drinker, another mystery must surely be how such a bizarre design for a puzzle jug came to be created by the Leeds potters in the first place. Usually about 15in: 380mm high, various versions, though basically the same, differed in detail, the perforated neck being sometimes as shown here, sometimes boat-shaped and sometimes resembling a flagon. The centre of the tyre-shaped body was always open-work in a variety of patterns and a small model animal or bird (a lion in the jug above) was invariably contained between the two halves. Of typically fine white pottery, this jug is decorated in silver resist and dates from 1814. Usually Leeds puzzle jugs were in over-all silver lustre, though some were decorated with enamel colours.*

(Courtesy, Winterthur Museum, from the Gutman Collection)

Plate 122. *A very fine silver resist jug on a blue ground. Inscribed Jinny Ashton 1810. Origin unknown, but probably Staffordshire.*
(Courtesy, Winterthur Museum, from the Gutman Collection)

the pottery they produced, and also for their whiteness, which gave great scope as a ground for silver and other resist lustre work. Probably clays from Dorset and Cornwall were also used.

Joshua Green went into partnership in 1775 with John Green of Hunslett 'and divers others to erect and maintain in repair at their mill and water-wheel with all necessary machinery for grinding flints…', the company trading as Humble, Green & Co. Thirteen years later Humble had retired and the name was changed, with the advent of William Hartley, to that by which it is properly known, Hartley, Greens and Co. This was to remain its title for about forty years, unusual in an industry where the more normal pattern was to fade away like melting snowflakes after a comparatively short existence. In fact the Greens themselves moved on (John to establish the Don Pottery), but the Leeds company continued under the hand of William Hartley. As mentioned earlier, Thomas Lakin was to join the Leeds company round about 1818, probably as manager of the decorating department, and finished his working life there.

We are fortunate in being able to say quite a bit about the wares that were produced by the Leeds Pottery, in part because a respectable number of surviving pieces were

marked and also because pattern books produced in 1783, 1785, 1786, 1794 and 1814 still exist. The text was in English, French and German, reflecting the very considerable export market for which the factory catered. Copies of the pattern books for 1783 and 1794 are in the Victoria and Albert Museum Library in London (where, if you wish to turn their pages, you are issued with a special pair of gloves), while the others are in Leeds Central Library. They go under the title *Designs of Sundry Articles of Queen's or Cream-coloured Earthenware, Manufactured by Hartley, Greens and Co., at Leeds Pottery: with a Great variety of other Articles. The same enamel'd, Printed or Ornamented with Gold to any Pattern; also with coats of Arms, Cyphers, Landscapes, &c.* Note the use by yet another firm of Wedgwood's trade name 'Queensware', though the standard of the wares put out by the Leeds Pottery itself was so high that it is difficult to see why they felt the need to cash in on another's prestige in this way.

In view of their dates, only the last of these catalogues has any mention of lustre decoration. It, however, makes use of the printing plates of earlier editions which do not show decoration and is far from specific as to which might be lustred. As already indicated, Leeds white earthenware, as well as their creamware, was ideal for resist lustre and the

Plate 123. *A loving cup (ht 5½in: 140mm) and mug (ht 3¼in: 82mm), both probably from Leeds.* *(Stoke City Museum and Art Gallery)*

factory took full advantage of this. By far the greater quantity was done in silver lustre, though there are fine examples of jugs decorated with pink resist work (see Colour Plate 142) and there was a certain amount of copper lustre as well. It must be said that not too many pieces of Leeds silver resist are marked, but it is still possible to identify many of them through known Leeds characteristics in the designs. From a set of three exceptionally fine Leeds silver resist jugs shown in Plate 119, the largest one is no less than 7⅛in (190mm) high.

A great many lustre pieces from this factory feature birds and animals, surrounded by exotic foliage (with two different sorts of flower on the one plant), and the birds on these jugs are characteristically rather stiff and angular. In fact the Leeds zoo tended towards the eccentric, a typical example being the factory's lion which could be straight out of the Wizard of Oz. This appears on a number of pieces, amiable-looking and so bow-legged that it is impossible to imagine it tackling anything larger than a mouse, let alone a wildebeest or zebra. One forms the centrepiece of the very fine oval silver resist charger in the Burnap Collection in the William Rockhill Nelson Gallery of Art in Kansas City, U.S.A., while others appear on Leeds jugs and bough pots (Plates 114 and 115). It is generally considered unique, but a rather similar lion does appear in silver resist on a bough pot illustrated in *Collecting Lustreware*. It is impressed BOTT & Co., a company from Lane End, Staffordshire.

Designs incorporating leaves of many sorts are also typical of Leeds resist work and by no means confined to the fruiting vines so beloved of nineteenth century potters. Certain Leeds trees are very distinctive, with dense heads of rounded leaves with a small squiggle in the centre of each which makes them resemble nothing so much as embryo tadpoles in frog-spawn. A jug with a distinctive leaf pattern appears as an illustration under the 'probably Leeds' banner in John and Baker's *English Lustre Pottery* (which illustrates some marked Leeds lustreware and some that can be fairly attributed to Leeds.). Plate 117 in the present book shows the design on another jug, which should mean that it is from the same source. So too would be the much smaller jug also in Plate 117. Definite confirmation that they both came from Leeds has not so far been forthcoming, but there is no reason at the moment to change the attribution.

Leeds puzzle jugs are, to coin a phrase, a thing apart. The one shown in Plate 121, from the Gutman collection in America, will show what I mean and show, too, the wild flight of imagination that inspired the potter who designed them. Not all are exactly the same, for the handles can vary, and the perforated top, sometimes jar-shaped, was also sometimes in the shape of a sauce boat. The bodies and the pedestal bases were more likely to be nearly the same.

There were other, more conventional, Leeds puzzle jug designs, some decorated over-all in silver lustre, rather than using the resist technique. Lustred candlesticks, goblets, loving cups, dishes, teapots, chestnut baskets (perforated

Colour Plates 138, 139 and 140. *Three views of a large jug with the most elaborate decoration of coloured transfer prints and free brush strokes of both pink lustre (which also decorates the rims and handle) and enamel colours. It is dedicated to the Oddfellows and the various elements contain some very worthy sentiments. Williams-Wood's* Transfer Printed Pottery and Porcelain *shows a print of Leeds origin similar to the main one on this jug, but it bears, in minute lettering, the inscription: T. BADDELEY • ENAMELLER • HANLEY. Hanley is of course in the Potteries. c.1820s. Ht 7½in: 191mm. Note; Oddfellows sometimes appears on pottery as one word and sometimes incorrectly as two. The organisation was said to have much in common with Freemasonry.*

Plate 124. *One of the very distinctive pink lustre flat-topped coffee pots produced by William Smith's Stafford Pottery at Stockton-on-Tees. They were made in a number of sizes and decorated in many different ways. This one is unmarked but a number can be found impressed, quite illegally, WEDGWOOD & CO, a practice to which William Smith was somewhat addicted.*

identical, so that his creamware had a greyish tinge and his glaze had a tendency to crazing. He reproduced a large part of the true Leeds Pottery range – figures, pierced ware of various sorts, tableware and so on – and, while these were well done, they lacked something of the feel of the real thing.

The products of Senior's factory were mostly marketed through a well-known Leeds antique dealer by the name of W.W. Slee, and it was he who put out the catalogue referred to above. Senior always claimed that he was perfectly in order in impressing what he produced as LEEDS ★ POTTERY but, as this marking cannot do other than confuse the uninitiated, this must remain open to question.

Colour Plate 146 shows three yellow-glazed pieces with silver lustre decoration made by Senior, all with the Leeds mark, about which I consulted Peter Walton, former Director and Curator of the Bar Convent Museum, York. He told me:

Senior is known to have made yellow-glazed ware and both the shapes and pattern are shown in W.W. Slee's catalogue of the Seniors' productions…the design was also manufactured in blue and white. The pieces shown in your photograph are 18th century Leeds Pottery shapes and incorporate 18th century moulded knobs and handle terminals. The teapot is a good reproduction of an 18th century piece. The milk jug and sugar are not.

Eighteenth century Leeds pottery would not, of course, have been decorated with lustre.

ware was a Leeds speciality) as well as a wide range of different jugs and other items were part of the overall picture.

Leeds marks took the form LEEDS ★ POTTERY, sometimes with the small star in the centre and sometimes not, or else the words HARTLEY, GREENS AND CO arranged in a circle, in both cases impressed. However, a warning must be given. A number of pieces are in circulation today bearing the first of these two marks which did not, in fact, come from the original Leeds factory. Early in the twentieth century James Wraith Senior, who had worked at Leeds, set up his own pottery in Hunslett to produce, with his two sons, what he described as a revival of Leeds Pottery manufacture. The catalogue of his products, dated 1913, stated that the patterns and moulds he was using were obtained from the old Leeds factory so that he was producing the genuine article, even though a good many years had elapsed since the closure of the original plant. However, his raw materials, in particular his clays, were by no means

Middlesbrough Pottery 1831-1887

This was on the east coast of Yorkshire near the mouth of the river Tees, not far from William Smith's Stafford Pottery. From its beginnings in 1831, through to 1844, the firm was known as the Middlesbrough Pottery Company, after which it became the Middlesbrough Earthenware Company. Finally, until its closure in 1887, it was Isaac Wilson & Co.

For the influence of Sunderland (not all that distant up the coast) on the Middlesbrough wares one need look no further than a set of plates decorated with transfers of prints specially prepared for the temperance movement by George Cruikshank in 1848. They show the gradual downfall of a family through the Demon Drink and are very similar to a set put out by Sunderland's Moore's Southwick Pottery. Cruikshank addressed the Mechanic's Institute in Middlesbrough in 1851 and Robert Bloore, manager of potting, was on the committee, so their meeting may have inspired the prints. Other Middlesbrough pieces, tablewares, vases, jugs, bowls and so on, when decorated with lustre, also closely resemble their equivalents from Wearside. Sometimes they are a little more sophisticated, but by no means always. The very appealing lustre-decorated children's plates with the well-known moulded daisy border, of which large quantities were produced, were probably more typical of the Tees than the Wear.

For some reason, an explanation of which has still to be found, the Middlesbrough Pottery sometimes used an impressed shield mark, in which was contained the word LONDON, in turn surmounted by an anchor. This mark has been found on plaques and on an 1820s bowl, which could easily have come from John Carr of Newcastle except for one thing. Both Newcastle and Middlesbrough, on otherwise identical bowls, used transfer prints of Brunel's ship *The Great Eastern,* but the Middlesbrough version carried the additional word 'Leviathan'.

Apart from the mark mentioned above, M.P. & CO and, later, I.W. & CO were quite often used.

The Stafford Pottery 1825-1870

The location of this company is always given as Stockton-on-Tees and the name Stockton is included in one of its makers' marks. Stockton is on the north side of the river Tees and in the county of Durham, so the fact that the Stafford Pottery belongs in the Yorkshire group needs explanation. It was, in fact, at Thornaby, just over the river on the south, the Yorkshire side, but it would seem that the larger, better-known Stockton adjoining it was considered the better business address. It was a firm that went all out for the export market and was highly successful in this field. Large quantities of their wares were sold in Belgium, Holland and Germany and a branch was actually established in Mons, with workers being sent over to Belgium to pass on their skills to the locally recruited workers. In addition there was a selling agency in Hamburg. Much white and brown earthenware was sent overseas in addition to that with lustre decoration.

The company was started in 1825 by William Smith, who wisely took into partnership a man, John Whalley, who had long experience of the pottery industry in Staffordshire, but the pair of them were none too scrupulous in their business practices. One set of Stafford Pottery marks incorporated the word QUEENSWARE, a name for a particular kind of Wedgwood pottery. In addition, Wedgwood had to take legal action to stop William Smith from actually marking some of his wares W.S. & CO WEDGWOOD WARE, W.S. & CO'S WEDGEWOOD, or simply WEDGEWOOD. The insertion of an E in the latter did not really hide the intention to deceive.

Plate 125. *A saucer from a large and attractive pink lustre tea set from the Stafford Pottery. It is beautifully decorated, each piece bearing a different rural scene, enhanced by enamel colours. Unfortunately, as was frequently done by William Smith, the pottery's owner, he has chosen, for reasons we can only guess at, to impress the pieces W.S. & Co's Wedgwood Ware. Later he changed the spelling of Wedgwood, adding an 'e', but this did not really make it any less misleading. c.1820s. Dia 5in: 125mm.* (Cockerill Collection)

The pink lustre child's plate in Colour Plate 144 is an example of the trouble that the Stafford Pottery took to match their goods to their overseas markets. The legend running round the top of the plate reads HAMBURG, ANSICHTEN (Views of Hamburg) and under the picture is DIE LOMBARDS BRUCKE (The Lombards Bridge). This plate is one design among many with daisy borders produced by William Smith, including a series depicting the months of the year. That the Stafford Pottery could when it tried produce works of real merit is shown by the very elegant coffee pot in the French style shown in Plate 124. It is not marked but others of the same pattern are almost certain to be from the Stafford works even though they bear the mark WEDGEWOOD.

Other Stafford Pottery marks included

W.S.& CO
QUEEN'S WARE
STOCKTON

and

S. & W.
QUEEN'S WARE
STOCKTON

the latter coming into effect from 1870, when the partnership of Skinner and Walker took control.

Colour Plate 141. *Contrast this Leeds chestnut basket with the one by Thomas Lakin in Colour Plate 66. They are much alike, but this one is more finely potted and decorated with purple lustre and red and green enamels over a biscuit-coloured slip. Stand impressed Hartley, Greens and Co. c.1820s. 10¼in: 260mm x 8½in: 216mm.*

Colour Plate 142. *A finely decorated jug in a mauvish-pink variant of pink resist lustre, a colour favoured by the Leeds Pottery. The rim and handle decoration is in blue enamel. c.1820. Ht. 5¼in: 133mm.*

Colour Plate 143. *The very distinctive shape of this coffee pot, with its flat top and recessed lid, suggests at once that William Smith's Stafford Pottery of Stockton-on-Tees was the maker. However, details of the spout, the finial, the spurs on the handle, and even the 'cottage'-style pink lustre decoration, raise doubts. It could be a copy, possibly from the Newcastle Tyne Pottery of Patterson and Co. c.1825-1830. Ht 10in: 254mm.*

Colour Plate 144. *One of the many designs of children's plates made by the Stafford Pottery and exported by them in great quantities. The inscription on this is in German, showing that it was made for that market, more specifically for Hamburg, where the firm had a selling agency. c.1825. Dia 6½in: 165mm.*

Colour Plate 145. *A silver resist lustre teapot, the shape and decorative design of which link it closely with several of the bough pots shown in this book, indicating that the maker, possibly Leeds, was the same. c.1820s. Ht 4½in: 114mm.*

Colour Plate 146. *A teapot, milk jug and sucrier, decorated with silver lustre on a yellow slip, each piece impressed LEEDS POTTERY. They are not, however, genuine early Leeds ware, but were made by James Wraith Senior, probably early in the 20th century, long after the original factory had ceased to exist.*

CHAPTER VIII

Other English Provincial Factories

This small group of potteries, widely distributed from Bristol in the south to Liverpool and Warrington in the north, all almost certainly made use of lustre decoration. Apart from the Herculaneum Pottery in Liverpool where the (rather vague) indications are that quite a quantity of lustreware was produced, they do not in general appear to have used this form of decoration widely. However, the wares from all of them are sufficiently different from the run of the mill to more than justify their inclusion here.

Bristol 1786-1855

Bristol is in rather an odd position in that its pottery at Brislington, just south-east of the town, was for long thought to have been an extensive producer of copper lustre wares, which it never was. Yet Bristol is scarcely known for the pink lustre it did produce later, albeit in small quantities. As recently as 1962, John and Baker, having demolished the copper lustre myth, could write: 'No lustred earthenware of any description was ever made at Brislington and furthermore, it is almost certain that typical English metallic lustres were not produced in recognizable quantities by the other later Bristol potteries'.

The first part of John's statement is no longer in dispute and the authors go into considerable detail as to how the misconception arose. A summary of their account of the unravelling of the mystery will be given shortly, for it takes us down one of the more interesting byways in the story of lustre. The second part of their statement does need amplification.

In Gibson and Godden's *Collecting Lustreware* true Bristol lustreware was recognised, possibly for the first time, and it was during research for this book that a few clues began to emerge. Identification was backed, not by a factory mark, but by the discovery of a group of pieces remarkable for their enamel decoration of a kind associated with a known Bristol decorator, on all of which pink lustre was also used. Some of them were also of known Bristol shapes and patterns, and they could be given an approximate date as they actually bore, usually on the base, the initials or the full

Plate 126. *A presentation loving cup that leaves no doubt as to its origin, the Bristol Pottery. The decorator was likely to have been William Fifield, using* enamel colours for his characteristic floral garlands, together with a pink lustre trim. 1842. Ht 4in: 102mm. *(Harris Museum and Art Gallery, Preston)*

Plates 127a and 127b. *A goblet or loving cup in pink resist lustre with details picked out in yellow, one of a number of such cups made to commemorate the visit of the Prince Regent to Coventry in 1811. One side shows the Elephant and Castle, forming the arms of Coventry, and the other* *the Prince of Wales' feathers, together with his motto, 'Ich Dien'. The name of the Mayor of Coventry, S. Vale, appears on both sides, together with the date, Oct., 1811. Unmarked, but both the style and the pink lustre resist would point to Liverpool manufacture.* (Gutman Collection)

name of William Fifield. He worked as senior decorator of creamwares for the Temple Backs Pottery in Bristol and specialised in floral decoration with great swags of roses and other flowers in over-glaze enamels. His style was most distinctive, only matched to some extent by that of his son, who also worked in Bristol. The father was at the pottery from c.1810-1855. Small spirit containers shaped like miniature barrels are well known as originating in Bristol and the British Museum has two in its pottery collection. The smaller one, 4⅛in (114mm) high, has typical coloured banding round the top and bottom with a decoration of flowers and butterflies in between. Pink lustre is included among the multicoloured concentric circles on the top and base of the barrel and the initials W.F. and date 1843 are grouped on a raised lozenge half way up the side where one would expect to find the bunghole. Even more noteworthy in the same collection is an oblong pottery trinket box, 7in (178mm) long by 4in (105mm) high, by 2½in (64mm) deep. Slots around the top on three of the sides would seem to indicate that at one time it had a sliding lid. One can only speculate how this may have been decorated, but each side of the box has floral decoration quite obviously by the same hand as the one that embellished the barrel. The box has a pink lustre trim and four pink lustre feet and on turning it over there is a real surprise. In running script there are the words:

Tho' a trifle this may seem,
'Tis a pledge of my esteem.
August 12th 1828 W. Fifield

Plate 128. *A pedestal vase, 4⅛in: 114mm high, attributed to Herculaneum. The cream-coloured body has fruiting vine silver resist decoration on its lower half, surmounted by a sepia transfer print of a harpist. c.1820.* (The National Museums and Galleries of Merseyside, Liverpool Museum)

Colour Plate 147. *A beautiful but unmarked puzzle jug, combining pink lustre and very muted and delicately applied enamel colours. The blue rim and blue trim on the handle and round the base are unusual. c.1830. Ht 6½in: 165mm.*

The Harris Museum and Art Gallery in Preston has another example of Fifield's lustre work, a 4in (102mm) high, tankard-shaped, pink lustre-banded loving cup (Plate 126). There can be absolutely no doubt of its origin, even though it only bears a hand-painted F. The floral decoration contains perhaps a larger selection of flowers than usual, roses, morning glory, nasturtiums and honeysuckle among them, and they form a reserve on one side in which are the following words in pink lustre:

A Present
From the
Bristol Pottery
1842

In none of these pieces is lustre used as the main decoration and it would seem that Bristol, in the person of William Fifield, regarded it as a useful and attractive adjunct to other decorating schemes. This theory is borne out by the Bristol creamware puzzle jug (Colour Plate 148) where the pink lustre is used only on the perforated neck. The jug is of a kind made in a number of sizes, from only about 4in (105mm) tall to the 6⅓in (165mm) example shown here. All seem to have been decorated with flowers, either by Fifield or his son in their clearly recognisable style, but the use of lustre on one of them is unusual. The initials W.F. in pink lustre are on the base and the front carries the following inscription in a flowing script:

Thomas and Sarah Wakefield
Sirhowy
Let us sing success to the Mines Of Iron and Coal

This is reminiscent, if rather more sophisticated in its presentation, of the legends to be found on the pottery from Sunderland and Newcastle, celebrating the local industries. Mining was carried out near Radstock, south of Bristol, but Sirhowy is over the Welsh border, near Ebbw Vale in the Welsh coalfields, and this was, presumably, where Thomas and Sarah Wakefield lived. Obviously it is a presentation piece, perhaps for their wedding and it is a pity there is no date. However, the jug probably comes from the 1840s.

Having established that there was at least some pink lustreware produced in Bristol, even if only by one very prolific family of decorators, it is time to return briefly to the Bristol copper lustre that never was.

In 1873 Hugh Owen published his *Two Centuries of Ceramic Art in Bristol* in which he described how copper lustre was first produced at the Brislington Pottery. He illustrated a copper lustre dish some 14in (356mm) in diameter, on the reverse side of which was what could be a monogram made up from the initials of Richard Frank, the man who took over the running of the pottery in its later days. Jewitt, writing a few years later, appears to accept

Colour Plate 148. *A pink lustre puzzle jug, from the Temple Backs Pottery, Bristol, decorated with floral sprays typical of their chief decorator, William Fifield, whose initials in pink lustre appear on the base. Pink lustre is also used on the neck and under the front spout are the words in a flowing script: 'Thomas & Sarah Wakefield, Sirhowy. Let us sing success to the Mines of Iron and Coal', making it possibly a marriage jug celebrating the union of two Welsh mining families. There is no date, but the 1830s would be about right. Ht 6½in: 165mm.*

Owen's word for it, though whether he had first-hand knowledge of the Brislington wares is uncertain. At any rate, he describes the Brislington patterns as: '…being of coarse and rude designs, in a kind of copper or red lustre, on a plain buff clay ground. Some good examples of this ware, which is clumsy and coarse, but curious, are preserved in the Bristol Museum.'

There the matter ended until an article appeared in *The Connoisseur* in June 1908. This was by Alfred Billson who, having closely examined the so-called Brislington lustreware in the Bristol Museum, had come to a pretty firm conclusion that it was imported Spanish earthenware which, as Bristol was a major seaport, was at least a distinct possibility. Billson's conclusions were to receive strong backing when W.J. Pountney published his *Old Bristol Potteries,* which included his account of the excavations of the site of the Brislington Pottery. Although shards of blue and white delft wares were found in plenty, there was not a trace of any lustre-decorated pieces. He also commented: '…I may mention that the local clays used at Brislington burnt to a light buff body, whereas that of the Spanish lustre body is of a dull brown red colour'. And we know that the Brislington Pottery had closed in 1775 on the death of Richard Frank, some thirty years before lustre of any kind was used on British ceramics.

The Temple Backs Pottery was established by Joseph Ring in 1786, which is the date on an invoice which gives a very good idea of the range of wares they produced. They included: 'Oval dishes of varying sizes, table plates, soups and suppers, twifflers, tureens, quart jugs…coffee cups bowles, quart mugs variegated and pint mugs variegated', and a good deal more. There was no mention at this time, it may be noticed, of puzzle jugs, trinket boxes or loving cups, but all must have come later, after the turn of the century, when the firm had become Carter and Pountney.

Caughley and Coalport 1775-1799 and 1799 to present
The Caughley factory, near Broseley in Shropshire, changed hands in 1799, John Rose and Co. taking over from Thomas Turner. They produced, in addition to their porcelains, a certain amount of dark-bodied earthenware, which they considered was made more acceptable by the use of a white slip, as seen, for example, on the coloured bodies from other manufacturers. In due course John Rose was to acquire the Coalport Porcelain Works and it was probably then that a different approach was decided on in order to make the dark-coloured Shropshire earthenware more saleable. A very deep-toned copper lustre was used as a ground, against which gilt classical figures and the extensive use of Greek key borders, also gilded, provided a striking contrast. It is believed that the same moulds were often employed for both porcelain and earthenware items and also that a gold-based purple lustre was used on a certain number of the wares from Coalbrookdale.

Plate 129. *This fine silver resist jug may be of Herculaneum origin. The inscription in the reserve reads 'Ex Dona of T. Hatton To William Halliday. Everton Coffee House', the latter being a well-known 19th century Liverpool meeting place. c.1815. Ht 7¾in: 197mm.*
(The National Museums and Galleries of Merseyside, Liverpool Museum)

It is far from easy nowadays to find any of these Caughley/ Coalport examples, though Colour Plate 150 shows a small dish from this factory. Other examples from this period can be seen in the Victoria and Albert Museum, London. A very similar decorative style on dark-coloured pottery was also used by David Wilson in Staffordshire but, fortunately from the point of view of attribution, the latter's wares were sometimes impressed with the maker's name.

The Herculaneum Pottery – Liverpool 1796-1841

This pottery, established in 1796 at Toxteth Park by a Liverpool corn merchant by the name of Samuel Worthington, has a reputation in its later period for very fine lustreware in copper, pink and silver, but it is extremely difficult to produce the evidence on which this reputation is built. In fact a good deal of the information we have casts considerable doubt on there being any lustre decoration at all. However, this information is of the negative kind, such as The Tomkinson Papers quoted in Alan Smith's *Illustrated Guide to Liverpool Herculaneum Pottery* in which long lists of the factory's output are given but lustre is nowhere mentioned.

There is some evidence, however, that Herculaneum lustreware did exist, but before going into details it might be as well to say a little more about the factory. The

manager was a Mr Mansfield, who came to Liverpool from Burslem to open the enterprise in 1796, bringing with him a substantial number of his fellow Staffordshire craftsmen and their families. Together they formed a colony with its own housing, very much on the lines of Wedgwood's at Etruria, though by no means all the Herculaneum workers who lived there came from Staffordshire. The factory grew and prospered, having, in the early days, taken on more staff from other, less successful, Liverpool firms.

The output covered the usual range of domestic wares, and creamware, for which Liverpool was to become famous, was developed. It was of a slightly darker shade than that of the Wedgwood factory and rather less yellow than that from Leeds. Extensive use was made of black transfer prints and bat printing for decoration. It would be strange indeed if such a go-ahead enterprise, which existed during the peak period for lustre decoration, did not at least dabble. There is a feeling that they did a good deal more than that, but clearly it is an area in need of much more research.

The Liverpool Museum ceramic collection would have seemed to be the place to start, but it is a disappointment. However, it has got a creamware jug and a mug in matching style with the same sepia print of a cottage on each, and with purple lustre trim (Plate 130). There is added lustre

Plate 130. *Bearing on their reverse sides the wording 'Cottage near Walton', the latter being a district of Liverpool, this jug and mug have identical rural transfer prints and copper lustre banding. c.1820. Jug ht 5in: 127mm and mug ht 3½in: 89mm.*
(The National Museums and Galleries of Merseyside, Liverpool Museum)

decoration on the jug. Both carry the legend 'Cottage near Walton', which is a district of Liverpool and, in the nineteenth century, a good deal more rural than it is nowadays. There is no mark, but it would seem likely that it was a local product. Probably the strongest circumstantial evidence for the production of finely executed lustreware in Liverpool is the silver resist jug shown in Plate 129. It is unlikely that a coffee house would go out of its own area to have this made.

Warrington 1797-1812
Jewitt draws our attention to the fact that Warrington had a factory which apparently escaped the eye of past researchers as a producer of lustreware. He wrote: 'Of the production of the works, my late friend Dr. Kendrick got together a number of examples, which he deposited in the Warrington Museum. The wares produced were an ordinary quality of white ware; blue and white printed goods, and both silver and gold lustre.' Dr Kendrick was a noted authority and clearly he was creating some kind of visual record of the output of a local industry. It was obviously important to him to establish just what was of local origin because a great deal of the output of the Warrington Pottery was much influenced by Staffordshire designs and closely resembled them. This was not surprising, for the manager at Warrington was one Joseph Ellis, who came to them from the Wedgwood factory, bringing with him a number of

workers from Hanley, who set up yet another potters' colony like the ones at Herculaneum and Etruria. None of the wares was marked, which has made Dr Kendrick's gift to the museum all the more valuable.

Warrington Pottery stood on a site known as Pottery Yard on Bank Quay, on the banks of the Trent and Mersey

Plate 131. *This jug, c.1810-1820, is probably from the Warrington Pottery. There is a broad copper lustre band edged by moulded beading round the neck, and a pink lustre spout and trim. The transfer print relates to the Independent Order of Oddfellows. Ht 5½in: 140mm.*
(Warrington Museum)

Colour Plate 149. *A jug with an unusual style of decorative mouldings of the Scottish thistle and English rose and a pink lustred rim, made by the Warrington Pottery. c.1810-1820. Ht 5½in: 140mm.*

Canal, and this location was one of the main reasons for its existence. Two brothers, James and Fletcher Bolton, noted the fact that the white clays from the West Country needed by the pottery industry in Staffordshire were shipped by sea to Liverpool and from there transported by barges on the canal to their final destination. The canal passed right through Warrington and, if they set up their own pottery and put in orders for Cornish clay themselves, unloading at Bank Quay would make for a shorter journey, with lower costs. This would enable them to compete on better than equal terms with their rivals further south, so they opened for business in 1797. Joseph Ellis was to join them not long afterwards and the firm ran reasonably successfully until 1812. He was particularly interested in the development of new colours, glazes and bodies and experimented with them in his spare time. During the fifteen years of its existence there must have been a considerable total output of wares of many kinds, many of them destined for the American market. Presumably today, many of them must still be in existence under that all-embracing term 'Staffordshire'. Without marks, identification is difficult, if not impossible, but the Warrington Museum still has the pieces that made up Dr Kendrick's gift.

Perhaps the most striking is illustrated in Colour Plate

Plate 132. *Another Warrington jug with a very distinctive design of neck. Strongly executed floral decoration in enamels is supported by pink lustre trim, top and bottom. c.1810-1812. Ht 7in: 178mm.*

(Warrington Museum)

Colour Plate 150. *A rare example of Coalport lustre, a fluted dish, the classical theme, including a Greek key border, in gold on a copper lustre background. c.1810.*
(Blakey collection)

Plate 133. *A Warrington Pottery plate boldly decorated in orange, blue, yellow and green enamels, combined with pink lustre. c.1810-15. Dia 10in: 254mm.* *(Warrington Museum).*

149, a 5½in (140mm) jug with relief moulding of a thistle and rose on the side, signifying the union of Scotland and England, brightened with coloured enamels and with pink lustre for the spout and lower banding. Other similar jugs can be seen occasionally in a range of sizes and they are very handsome. The museum also has another jug carrying a transfer print of a symbol representing The Ancient Order of Oddfellows, with a copper lustre top and pink lustre bottom banding (Plate 131). There is a plain, looped handle in the Sunderland style and the jug could easily have come from almost any pottery in the country.

Much more distinctive is yet another 7in (178mm) jug (Plate 132) which has quite an elaborate moulded handle with a distinctive curlicue at the top attachment point and an unusual decorated bulge in the pottery just below the rim, a feature unique, as far as is known, to Warrington. The rim has pink lustre decoration, as has the foot-rim, and the remaining decoration is a freely painted confection of flowers and leaves in bright blue, yellow, orange and green enamels. A 7in (178mm) diameter plate in the museum has the same basic colour range in addition to pink lustre and, almost inevitably, there are some Gaudy Welsh pieces. Silver lustre has one representative, a not very well executed silver resist goblet. There do not appear to be any known marks.

165

CHAPTER IX

Scottish Lustreware

In comparison with England, the pottery industry was late in establishing itself north of the border. This is not really surprising, for Scotland, in the seventeenth century and earlier, was a country with its economy based on sheep farming and fishing. Much of it was ruled (I use the word advisedly) by the owners of vast estates and security of tenure was often very precarious. Thus industries, such as the domestic production of fine woollen cloth, were of the kind that could be moved from place to place relatively easily, even if in some cases reluctantly, but a pottery, with its kilns, crushing mills and other buildings, was a very different matter. As we know, many potteries depended on local sources of clay and would have been bereft without them.

In addition, there was the question of a market for what a pottery produced. By far the greater part of the country was sparsely populated and the crofters, making their livings in the highlands, often lived there in very primitive conditions in which anything as fragile as pottery could expect only a short life. Wooden vessels were much more practical and were normal for everyday use.

Taking all this into account, it is logical that, when the use of pottery gradually became more general, the factories tended to be in the populated areas on the banks of the Clyde in and down river from Glasgow, where ship building had already created an industrial climate, or else on the southern side of the Firth of Forth, just to the east of Edinburgh. The Caledonian Pottery, J. & M.P. Bell Ltd., the Clyde Pottery at Greenock, the Annfield Pottery, and the much later Britannia Pottery were five of the Glasgow firms, and important manufacturers of the Edinburgh area were Portobello, the Gordon Pottery of Prestonpans, and the Alloa Pottery, much closer to the city centre than the others. A number of these, with the help of skilled workers brought north from Staffordshire, grew into substantial businesses, not least in the export market to which the two rivers gave them easy access. None, however, was to become a household name in the way that Spode, Minton or Wedgwood did south of the border. All except the Britannia Pottery of 1860 were established in the late eighteenth century, so that they could not, in their early years, have been users of lustre decoration.

That silver, pink and copper lustre was used in Scotland is beyond dispute, but it seems to have arrived very late in the day, probably not much before the 1840s or 1850s. Which kind, and just how much of it was used by the different firms, it is impossible to say with any certainty due to the usual lack of factory marks, though it is possible to pick up clues here and there. One thing is certain, however, and that is that a great deal of use was made of orange lustre, that with a soft yellow tinge derived from iron oxide. A wash of this was applied, not as the main decoration, but as the background to coloured transfer prints, or perhaps for the edging on bowls or jugs.

J. Arnold Fleming's *Scottish Pottery*, published in 1923, is a book which any researcher must read to obtain a good over-all picture. It is always held to be not entirely

Plate 135. *The printed mark of the Glasgow potters J. & M.P. Bell is on the reverse of this plate, decorated in their 'Warwick Vase' pattern in a pink transfer print embellished with purple lustre, c.1850. Dia 11in: 279mm.* *(Glasgow Museums and Art Galleries)*

reliable, though in what way no-one seems to be prepared to say! At any rate it has in it a picture of the Scottish copper lustre version of the well-known 'polka' jug and places it as a product of the Alloa factory though it was based, as we know, on the design by George Ray of Longton in Staffordshire (see Chapter IV). The moulding has, however, as was usually the case with copies, lost some of its crispness, the mould itself having presumably been made from an existing jug imported for the purpose. Copper lustre also came from the Caledonian Pottery in Glasgow, while the Gordon Pottery in Prestonpans could be the original home of a small copper lustre jug in the Glasgow Museum, which has a moulded mark incorporating a 'G'. Several guesses have been made as to what the 'G' stands for, including, at its simplest, the town of Glasgow. On the other hand the letter and the lines surrounding the letter are to be found cut into the corner stones of Masonic halls. Perhaps there was one in Prestonpans.

Despite the general lack of factory marks, other evidence has been pieced together to make it almost certain that copper, pink and orange lustre was used in all the main Scottish whiteware potteries including, in addition to those already mentioned, the Bo'ness, the Kirkcaldy and East Lothian. Orange lustre was used by Annfield, Verreville, the Victoria Pottery, Pollockshaws, Clyde Pottery, McNay's Pottery and the Fife Pottery, and it is with the late orange lustre wares from all sources that it is possible to make some positive identifications, which cannot be done on the

earlier pieces. A number actually have a maker's name printed on the base, and there are registered decorative designs. Very typical of Scottish orange lustreware in general were the flask-shaped, quite heavily potted jugs and countless rather handsome punchbowls, with or without a pedestal foot.

Alloa Pottery, Fife 1790-

This was one of the earlier Scottish potteries, being established in 1790, long before the coming of lustre decoration. Early on the firm concentrated on fairly basic earthenware pans and crocks, using local clays. Fifty years later it was discovered, after W. & J. Bailey had taken over, that this clay was ideal for the making of majolica, a form of ceramics that was pioneered in Scotland by Alloa. Other of Bailey's lines were 'Rockingham-style' teapots and jugs, while some copper lustre in Glasgow Museum has been attributed to him, though with the usual lack of firm evidence that is such a part of the Scottish scene. Jewitt records that something like 20,000 teapots could be produced a week and that a speciality of the firm was the engraving of ferns and other decorations on their best lines, enhanced by a glaze in which 'the density of colour and softness of touch are highly commendable'.

Annfield Pottery, Gallowgate 1896-

This short-lived pottery was one of a number set up by John Thomson in 1896 to manufacture both china and earthenware. To help to run it, a work force was introduced

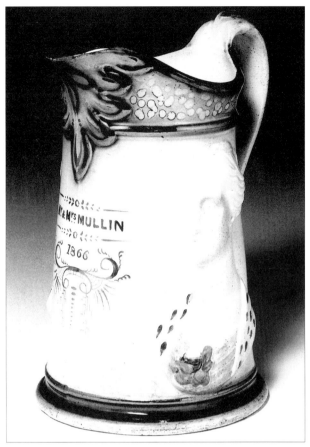

Plate 136. *Mottled pink lustre and copper lustre banding and trim, all on a blue ground, distinguish this Portobello Pottery jug. c.1866. Ht 8in: 203mm. (Glasgow Museums and Art Galleries)*

from Burslem in Staffordshire. Good quality white earthenware tea services decorated with mulberry transfer prints of oriental scenes were exported in quantities abroad and were popular in Australia. Some lustre decoration was probably used. Occasional makers' marks, with the pattern name contained in a garter, were:

JT & S   JT   JT & SONS   THOMSON   APJT
    ANNFIELD   GLASGOW   (Impressed)

Bo'ness Pottery 1766-1889

Established in 1766 at Borrowstouness, of which Bo'ness is a contraction, this was another of the earlier Scottish ceramic companies and was primarily intended for the manufacture of common brownwares for the domestic market. In 1784, however, things changed when a Dr John Roebuck bought the factory and updated it so that, using clays brought from the south of England, high quality creamware, white stoneware and slipware could be manufactured to compete with the best. The range, covering domestic wares in the main, was wide and included chimney ornaments and statuettes of animals and birds. Their 'Bosphorus' pattern is one of their best known and there is a fine orange lustre punchbowl from Bo'ness in the Glasgow Museum. Decorators from Staffordshire

were employed but, though the factory was to become one of the largest potteries in the country, it finally closed its doors in 1889.

Britannia Pottery 1860-1920

This company was established in a large works at St Rollox, Glasgow, in 1860 by Robert Cochran, who was a senior partner in the Verreville Pottery, also in Glasgow (q.v.). He was to be succeeded by his son, Alexander, and James Fleming. In 1896, the name of the firm was changed to Cochran and Fleming, but by 1911 it had reverted to Fleming alone. The first Cochran was quick to see how the American market might expand with the end of the Civil War and produced very durable ironstone wares that were eminently suitable for the rigours of export across the Atlantic, and the possibility of an additional trek by ox waggon across Indian territory to the West. South America was also a good market for the Britannia Pottery.

As for the wares themselves, these included much for ordinary domestic use, with quite a range of jugs including a three-spout puzzle jug. Their 'Ceres' pattern, which remained popular for about fifteen years, and was made up of moulded wheatsheaves with under-glaze colouring, was actually designed for them by David Chetwynd of Hanley in Staffordshire. It was used on a number of pieces and was a great favourite in South America. As for lustre, one example is a wall plaque dating from the 1870s which, though unmarked, bears the well-known Britannia 'Duchess' pattern, based on a Gainsborough painting. The rim is decorated in orange lustre.

The company carried on into the twentieth century but, after a buy-out by the Britannia Pottery Company in 1920, concentrated on what they called semi-porcelains. Earlier marks might be C. & F.G. FLEMING (impressed or printed), C. & F. ENGLAND (not Scotland) or, between 1896 and 1920, a printed figure of Britannia, including the pattern name and the word COCHRAN underneath.

Caledonian Pottery c.1780-

This pottery, established c.1780 by Robert Reid and Archibald Paterson, went through several changes of name and location during the course of its life. From a start in Glasgow, it moved, under new ownership and the new name of Murray & Co., to Rutherglen, about two miles distant from the old works. According to Jewitt, 'at first fine porcelain and china were made; then cream-coloured printed ware, with Rockingham and salt-glazed wares'. In 1851 the demand sprang up for stoneware ale and other bottles, and these were to become one of the staple trades of Glasgow and the surrounding district. Jewitt does not mention lustre decoration, but there are pieces of over-all copper lustre which can fairly confidently be attributed to the Caledonian. Among these is a teapot in a private collection with a very distinctive handle in the form of a bird. It is not actually marked but, on the occasions when a mark was used it took the form of a lion, impressed.

In 1807 the firm was taken over by Aitchison & Co., becoming known, for the first time, as the Caledonian

Colour Plate 151. *This moulded jug carries the impressed mark of J. & M.P. Bell of Glasgow, and the design was registered in 1867. The fishmarket scenes in enamel colours reflect one of the industries of this northern port. The rim of the jug is in orange lustre. Ht 7½in: 191mm.*

Pottery. From 1867 production was almost entirely concentrated on stoneware flasks, jugs, statuettes and other domestic pieces, many with hunting scenes or well-known Scottish characters as moulded decoration.

Clyde Pottery, Greenock 1816-1903
There are quite a number of wares that, even without makers' marks, can quite confidently be attributed to this company, which was formed in 1816 under the management of Andrew Muir & Co. One of these is a round wall plaque (Plate 134) with orange lustre used for the rim and some of the background. The purple-coloured transfer print is known as the Clyde 'French' pattern and shows a harvest scene of some sort, though it is difficult to tell whether of grapes in a vineyard or hops. A man and a woman are the main subject of the picture, the man

wearing corn-stalks in his hat. There are more worked into the bridle of the horse, so perhaps it is a corn harvest but, whatever it is, the pair's rather exotic costumes make it unlikely that they are Scottish workers.

Though never used, as far as is known, in conjunction with lustre, 'Lily of the Valley' was among the most popular decorative patterns from the Clyde Pottery. It appeared extensively, however, in conjunction with Clyde spongeware, which was aimed at a higher quality market than the more popular lines. Greenock House, where pottery from the Clyde factory is on display, demonstrates the use of orange lustre on punchbowls, on distinctive jugs with their twisted handles and on many other products of the 1860s and 1870s.

By c.1830 Thomas Shirley had taken over the factory from Andrew Muir and the company mark (when it was

Plate 137. *The printed mark, Lockhart & Co., shows that this typical Scottish punchbowl came from the Victoria Pottery, Glasgow. It is decorated with the company's 'Richmond' pattern, consisting of a purple transfer print of fruit with added enamel colours. c.1860.*

(Glasgow Museums and Art Galleries)

used) became TS & CO. From then on it had a number of owners who continued to run things much as before, Ireland having become a particularly profitable market, aided possibly by a fairly brief link with the Larne Pottery. A later mark was C.P. & CO., either printed or impressed.

Glasgow Pottery 1842-

One might almost think on reading the following that Llewellynn Jewitt was the newly-appointed publicity manager of J. & M.P. Bell, established in Stafford Street, Glasgow, in 1842. Of it, he wrote:

> These works, established for the manufacture of white and printed earthenware, soon rose to the first rank among the potteries of Scotland. Later on the manufacture of china was commenced and later still the fine white and pearl granite wares, and white decorated sanitary wares…dinner, breakfast, tea, toilet, dessert and other services…from the plain white or cream colour to the most richly enamelled and gilt patterns. The earthenware services are of more than average excellence of quality, the china, both body and glaze, of superior class. Some of the dessert plates, with hand-painted groups of flowers and open-work rims, equal to most English makes; while some of the tea services are of tall classic form and of excellent taste in colour and decoration. In Parian admirable vases with figures in relief, and other ornamental goods are produced.

Bell's was certainly in the front rank and some of the products very fine, an example being a 11in (279mm) plate, dating from about 1850, in Glasgow Art Gallery and Museum and decorated with a Bell's 'Warwick Vase' transfer

pattern in pink and with purple lustre embellishments (Plate 135). It bears the company's printed mark, so there is no doubt as to its origin and it is one of the few positively identified pink/purple lustre Scottish pieces. Also in the museum is a Glasgow Pottery moulded commemorative jug, celebrating the marriage of the Prince of Wales and Princess Alexandra. The Prince of Wales' feathers are moulded under the spout and busts of the pair on either side.

The pottery moulded jug in Colour Plate 151 is from the Bell Brothers' factory, too. This reflects the Glasgow fishing industry, for there was a large fleet of drifters based at the port, part of the general seafaring tradition of the Clyde area. The jug has a broad base and is quite heavily potted. It is of a design registered by Bell's in 1876, with fisherfolk and a large creel of fish moulded into the body and coloured with bright enamels and an orange lustre trim. At about the same period the company produced large quantities of punch bowls, jugs and other domestic items bearing their 'British and Foreign Birds' pattern. They also made extensive use of flow blue in conjunction with pink and purple lustre.

Factory marks generally were made up from a printed pattern with the letters J. & M.P.B. & CO. underneath. Later they were impressed and depicted a bell in conjunction with various other combinations of the Bell company initials.

Gordon's Pottery, Prestonpans ?-1837

This one can probably be dismissed quite briefly in our review of lustre-producing Scottish potteries, if only because it closed its doors in 1837 at about the time that lustre decoration was to arrive this far north. Nevertheless, there is some evidence that orange lustre was used on their series of jugs depicting Jacobite themes. And there is, at least as a possibility, the copper lustre jug mentioned on page 167 as being in the Glasgow Museum.

Portobello Pottery, Prestonpans 1770-1850

This was the most easterly of the Edinburgh group of potteries on the southern edge of the Firth of Forth where it widens out and flows into the North Sea. The rather un-Scottish name was said to originate with the celebration of Admiral Vernon's victory over the Spanish at Puerto Bello in Panama in 1739, but as the founding of the company did not take place until over thirty years later in 1770, there must, I feel, be a question mark against this. Celebrations do not usually go on that long. Relief-moulded white, salt-glaze stoneware was an early special line, bottles, jars, jugs, foot and carriage warmers and spirit bottles were some of the products to which were added tiles and bricks and ordinary brown pottery in due course. By 1789 the firm was run by William Jameson, who extended the pottery and the range of wares to include pearlware, creamware and a varied range of chimney ornaments.

In his *Scottish East Coast Potteries 1750-1840,* Patrick McVeigh demolishes the myth, given wide credence after the publication of Arnold Fleming's *Scottish Pottery* in 1923, that the Portobello factory was at one time leased to 'Scott Bros.' This name has been found on at least one lustred piece (a mug) apparently emanating from Scotland and led for a time to confusion with Scott Bros. of Sunderland.

With the seemingly inevitable see-saw prosperity of pottery firms, Portobello closed for a couple of years about 1793, but then rose again, phoenix-like, from the ashes of its kilns. Run by Cookson and Jardine of Edinburgh until 1808, it changed hands again when Thomas Yoole and his brother-in-law and noted potter, Thomas Rathbone, took over. This began a period noted for the production of ornaments in wide variety, including Florentine lions and other more domestic animals, together with wall plaques in bright enamel colours, though it was a little too early for lustre to be employed. The latter came after another period of closure, this time for seven years, after which the company was once again revived. With this revival came a change of name to the Midlothian Stoneware Potteries. Now run by Dr W.A. Gray, it put out a range of toddy jugs and bowls, making use of splashed pink and copper lustre and the inevitable orange lustre.

Something else that could only have come from a Scottish pottery is the traditional 'luggie' or porringer, and it is known that slip-decorated reproductions of these were made in the mid- to late 1800s. Victoria Bergensen shows a pink lustred luggie in her *Price Guide,* p. 494, and places it with the Portobello pottery. It probably dates from the mid-1800s.

Verreville Pottery, Glasgow -1820

Said to be the first factory in Scotland at which china was produced, this pottery began life in 1777 as a glass works. It continued as such under the management of John Geddes until, in 1820, he started to produce earthenware as well. By 1835 the factory had changed hands and, now under the guidance of Robert Alexander Kidston, skilled potters, gilders and other workers were brought north from such illustrious ceramic centres as Derby and Coalport. China became an important addition to the Verreville range. Figures, porcelain basketwork and beautifully modelled flowers all appeared in the new medium, produced by a staff from the best training grounds.

In 1846 Kidston was succeeded by Robert Cochran, already encountered as a senior partner in the Britannia Pottery, who spent much money modernising the kilns and then, rather surprisingly, decided to cease the manufacture of china and concentrate on earthenware. There must have been a sound business reason for this, a possibility being that, despite the high quality that was a hallmark of the Verreville company, the market had yet to accept Scottish manufacturers as serious producers of the more refined wares.

A creamware mug with pink lustre banding in the

Plate 138. *Here the once-popular flow-blue enamel and copper lustre are combined, one might think inappropriately, to highlight the moulded foxgloves. This jug is known to be Scottish but the maker is uncertain. c.1860. Ht 8in: 203mm.* (Glasgow Museums and Art Galleries)

Glasgow Museum is thought to be of Verreville ware and rather resembles a Sunderland piece with its black transfer prints of shipping. Orange lustre was also used extensively almost to the end of the century. The only known Verreville factory marks consist of the occasional use of the initials of the various owners.

Victoria Pottery, Glasgow 1855-1864

Situated at Pollockshaws, this was established in 1855 and run by David Lockhart and Charles Arthur until the partnership dissolved with the resignation of the latter in 1864. Like most of the other Scottish companies, orange lustre was the staple background decoration for transfer printed designs and as an additional decoration on spongeware. Manufacture was concentrated on tableware and chimney ornaments. The Glasgow Art Gallery and Museum has a Victoria Pottery punchbowl in the factory's 'Richmond' pattern, a coloured transfer print in purple, under the glaze, showing a selection of autumn fruit (Plate 137). The background is orange lustre and the factory mark LOCKHART & CO. Other marks included L & A, DL & CO., DL & SONS, all impressed, and L & CO., D.L.S. & S and LOCKHART & ARTHUR, printed.

Colour Plate 152. *A jug dating from c.1923-1928 decorated by the factory of A.E. Gray and, according to printed wording on the base, made exclusively for William Whiteley's store in West London. The decorator's mark also tells us that Gray's own special 'Gloria' lustre was used. Ht 5¾in: 146mm.*

Colour Plate 153. *A bone china muffin dish decorated by A.E. Gray of Hanley. The decorative scheme, carried out in pink lustre and green and yellow enamels echoes that used about 100 years earlier by Staffordshire potters (see jug in Colour Plate 12) rather than the company's more usual mock Sunderland ware. The galleon mark in yellow and black used by Gray gives a date of between 1921 and 1931 and has the additional wording: 'T. Goode & Co., South Audley St., London W.' on the base, obviously the retailer for whom it was specially made. Dish dia 8in: 205mm.*

Colour Plate 154. *A very striking coffee set from A.E. Gray, to a design carried out by Susie Cooper, c.1928, and carried out in Gray's own Gloria Lustre.* *(Sotheby's)*

Colour Plate 155. *A striking group of ceramic designs by William De Morgan showing this artist/designer at his peak. c.1890.* *(Sotheby's)*

CHAPTER X

Lustre in the Twentieth Century

This book is primarily concerned with lustrewares of the nineteenth century but, as it is a continuing story, albeit one in which the peak of achievement was passed somewhere around 1860, some brief account of later production would seem to be desirable to complete the picture.

Gradually, as the nineteenth century drew to a close, enthusiasm for lustred wares grew less. The novelty of a glittering metallic finish had to some extent worn off as, probably, had some of the lustre itself. So much of it was applied to household wares that were in constant use that the vulnerability of the thin metal coating to regular and probably none too careful cleaning would have been exposed. Commercial pressures, too, brought on by competition from cheaper imports and the siphoning off of skilled workers into the many new industries that were springing up, led to a reduction in the standard. Many of the established potteries that made use of lustre closed their doors, or at least greatly reduced or even dropped lustre production.

Nevertheless there were some that carried on, perhaps

the most notable being the Wedgwood concern. Others included the firms of Allerton, and Maling in Newcastle upon Tyne, though the latter changed tack to some degree. They began to concentrate on the reduced pigment lustre, in which the results are much more difficult to predict as quite a small variation in the temperature of the kiln or the firing time or, indeed, the exact composition of the metals used, can make a considerable difference to the results. Very striking effects can come from this process and it was, and still is today, much favoured by the studio potters, whose principal aim is to produce novel (and sometimes strikingly beautiful) ceramics rather than uniform pieces. The Maling company were, nevertheless, successful in using this type of lustre as a commercial proposition, manufacturing a wide range of sets of tableware, ornaments and other decorative items, most of them marked with the Maling name. Though not by any means rare, they are sought after today by collectors.

It was this kind of Hispano-Moresque, reduced pigment lustre, that seemed to gain in popularity as the other kind lost ground – not that it ever, in its most exciting and exotic forms

Plate 139. *The maker of this striking silver lustre-decorated jug is unknown, but it is very much in the style of the 1930s. Ht 6in: 152mm.*

Plate 140. *An Alfred Powell designed silver lustre Wedgwood teapot from the same set as the milk jug shown on the right in Plate 141. c.1930s.*

in the hands of the artist potters, achieved widespread production. It did not always appeal to the mass market customers but, from the early part of the twentieth century onwards, it was produced in sufficient quantities to form rather more than just a sideline in the story of ceramic design.

In essence, this kind of lustring consists of pigments from metallic compounds, mixed with clay or ochre, and then applied to the surface of a pot or dish that has already been glazed and fired. Re-firing is carried out to soften the glaze, on which a thin metallic film is deposited if the oxygen in the kiln is reduced. For fuller information on this kind of lustre the collector cannot do better than read Alan Caiger-Smith's *Lustre Pottery* which, despite its title, really only covers this one process in any detail.

Going back briefly to the nineteenth century, by far the most important and influential figure working with iridescent lustre was William De Morgan (Colour Plate 155). Beginning in Chelsea in 1872, he worked on his own for some years, learning the craft as he went and developing his own very special style of decoration, for which he is still admired today.

However, he found that the unpredictability of the process was such that, while as often as not it produced results of great beauty, the proportion of failures was sufficiently high to make an unacceptable hole in his profits. He needed a partner in the business to share the load, and Halsey Richards joined him in 1888, when new kilns and workshops were opened in Fulham.

Plate 141. *Two Wedgwood milk jugs from the 1940s-50s. That on the left has a modern gold-brown lustre; the central one is decorated with silver lustre and Wedgwood's 'Ferrara' pattern and bears, both impressed and painted, the mark WEDGWOOD, BARLASTON; the third, right-hand jug, in silver lustre, is to a design by Alfred Powell, who, with his wife, carried out a number of Wedgwood designs in the 1930s.*

Colour Plate 156. *A very elegant and attractive silver lustre teapot bearing both the impressed and the printed mark of Gibson and Sons, the latter indicating that it was made c.1950.*

Colour Plate 157. *A cylindrical copper lustre ice pail with a difficult-to-see dark blue decorative frieze round the top and a cane handle, probably from Staffordshire in the late nineteenth or early twentieth century. Ht 5¼in: 133mm.*

Colour Plate 158. *A footed bowl in Wedgwood's Fairyland Lustre developed early in the 20th century following the designs of Daisy Makeig-Jones. The scenes from fairyland and from traditional fairytales so often depicted gave this type of lustre its name.* *(Sotheby's)*

Plate 142. *Very finely decorated in silver resist, and printed and impressed with the Minton mark, this earthenware teapot, cup and saucer date from the mid-1920s.*

The Pre-Raphaelite school of artists, in particular Edward Burne-Jones and William Morris, were now part of his circle and their work had an influence on his style. Primarily he was a designer rather than a potter, and many of his designs can be seen in collections in the Victoria and Albert Museum, the William Morris Gallery, Walthamstow, Leighton House, Kensington and at Kelmscott Manor out in the country near Lechlade in Gloucestershire. Collectors must pay a high price for William De Morgan-decorated pottery, which does come on to the market from time to time.

Another important name in the field of reduced pigment lustre at the very end of the nineteenth century was Pilkington, the family owning the Royal Lancastrian Pottery at Clifton Junction in Manchester. From the successful production of decorative tiles, they had progressed, from about 1904 onwards, to much more ambitious decorative vases, dishes, platters, ornaments and other domestic wares. Oriental themes were frequently used and they employed artist-designers of the calibre of Walter Crane, C.F.A. Voysey, W.S. Mycock and Gordon M. Forsyth, who was their Chief Artist from 1905 until 1920. Their work embodied the very best of Art Nouveau, in the period immediately before the First World War, which could be said to be the heyday of the firm. But, imaginative and beautiful as much of their work undoubtedly was, for some reason it never came to be ranked with that of De Morgan.

After the war, many of the leading figures in the company had either died or retired. It seemed that the heart had gone out of the business and, though production continued, albeit with a gradual reduction of lustred works, the end finally came in 1938 when the factory was closed

down. Good examples of Royal Lancastrian lustreware can be seen at the Victoria and Albert Museum, London, the Whitworth Gallery, Manchester, Manchester Art Gallery and the Harris Museum and Art Gallery, Preston.

The work of Edward Gray is discussed fairly fully in Chapters III and IV, which deal with reproductions of earlier wares, and the point is made that A.E. Gray & Co. was responsible for a great deal of original lustre decoration (Colour Plates 152 to 154). Much of it was of very high quality by designers of the status of Susie Cooper, who joined the firm as a young artist in 1922. Their lustre was not of the reduced pigment kind, the company buying in blank, ready-glazed whitewares from such firms as Denby, Crown Devon and Whieldon and Bursley. It was never itself a producer of pottery, and sometimes the original makers' marks can be discerned under the very distinctive ship design that Gray's used to identify their products. This did vary in detail over the years but remained basically the same. However, between 1930 and 1945 an Egyptian Pharoah's boat was used as a mark. Another design, showing the rays of the rising sun, ran from 1923 to 1928, but only on Gray's Gloria Lustre, which had a formula known only to themselves.

Wedgwood lustrewares from the twentieth century are touched on briefly under the factory entry in Chapter IV, this great company being one of the few to have carried on producing right through from the very early days. Their outstanding Fairyland Lustre appeared in the twentieth century, though production of this was always very limited (Colour Plate 158). Otherwise, in more recent times, lustre (primarily silver) has formed but one constituent of designs incorporating other decoration or been used most attractively for the rims of porcelain tearwares, for banding and so on. It may make up a very small part of the total decoration but it is used very skilfully to point up the various designs in which it is used. The husband and wife team of Alfred and Louise Powell were two among the distinguished team of lustre decorators under contract to Wedgwood until the death of Louise in 1956, Alfred carrying out the design of the pottery itself as well as of its decoration.

Lustre was used post-war on Royal Doulton patterns and by John Aynsley and Sons Ltd. of Longton and numerous others. Gibson & Sons and the Harvey Potteries in Burslem were two that used silver lustre during the same period, as often as not in a style that imitated the old Georgian silver tea services. Their potting, however, was heavy and clumsy compared to most, and the lustre not particularly well done. Another firm that made some attempt in the early days of the twentieth century to imitate the traditional was James Kent.

An important name in the story of post-war lustre is that of Wade. The Wade group of potteries came about in 1919 through the amalgamation of a number of companies run by members and friends of the one family, trading as George Wade & Son Ltd. At that time, and for some years afterwards, concentration was on industrial ceramics, but in 1927 the emphasis began to change with the introduction of Art Deco figurines, and in 1938 the firm branched out with the formation of Wade Heath & Co Ltd., at the Royal Victoria Pottery in Burslem. This was for the production of earthenware tableware, while the older company continued turning out tiles and fireplace surrounds.

From the mid-1930s onwards up to the Second World War a very considerable range of copper lustre ware was produced by Wade, the designs mostly based on those from the previous century. Though they were in many cases close reproductions of earlier works, including almost inevitably

Plate 143. *An earthenware pink lustre cup and saucer in the 'London' shape, the saucer impressed WEDGWOOD. c.1930. Ht 2½in: 64mm.*

George Ray's 1856 Polka Jugs, they were generally back-stamped WADE HEATH ENGLAND, which put them squarely where they belonged, in the twentieth century. Though the moulding might be the same, the over-all decorative treatment of many of them differed from their nineteenth century counterparts, in that copper lustre was used primarily as trim over a wide variety of coloured slips – a favourite being buff-yellow. A range of Toby jugs was a popular line, together with plates, teapots, cigarette boxes and a multitude of other things. Lustre production was revived briefly after the last war but, failing to find a worthwhile market, ceased in 1980. To the discerning eye, Wade copper lustre had a distinct tint of bronze, which distinguished it from that of the nineteenth century.

Of other companies that produced appreciable quantities of lustreware in this century one might mention John Beswick of Longton, though their main concentration was the modelling of small animals. Their factory mark was BESWICK ENGLAND and they are now part of the Doulton group of companies. Most of their lustre was copper, but it is true to say that the majority of companies nowadays prefer to use silver lustre on the better quality teawares and similar domestic china. The lustres, unlike those of the nineteenth century, are made up by specialist firms which supply them to the potteries ready prepared.

The large numbers of what are known as studio potters who today specialise in lustre decoration, following in the steps of William De Morgan, are artists with their own studios and kilns. Either as individuals, or sometimes in partnerships of two or three, they produce limited editions of specially designed (and usually very expensive) wares, but they are really outside the scope of this book. Those wanting to know more will find them comprehensively covered in Victoria Bergensen's *Encyclopedia of British Art Pottery*, and quite fully in Geoffrey Godden and Michael Gibson's *Collecting Lustreware*. There are also numbers of other books on the work of individual potters.

Plate 144. *In the artist-potter tradition, an earthenware dish with sgraffito decoration by Julia Carter Preston. 1987.*
(The National Museums and Galleries of Merseyside, Liverpool Museum)

Colour Plate 159. *From the studio pottery school, a very beautiful iridescent lustre bowl designed and decorated by Moira Forsyth, working at St Oswald's Studios, London, c.1930, before she decided to concentrate on working with glass rather than ceramics. She was the daughter of Gordon Forsyth, designer for the Royal Lancastrian Pottery. Her initials, in monogram form, are painted on the base of the bowl.*

Colour Plate 160. *A group of vases and a charger typical of the very fine designs by leading ceramic artists of the day which characterised the work of Pilkington's Royal Lancastrian Pottery just before the 1914-1918 war.* (Sotheby's)

Colour Plate 161. *A teapot decorated in silver lustre, bearing the printed mark of James Sadler & Sons in a decorative scroll surmounted by a crown, which indicates a c.1947 date. The firm was founded in Burslem in 1899 and teapots were its speciality. Ht 6in: 152mm.*

Colour Plate 162. *A coffee pot in silver resist lustre to the same pattern as the teaset in Plate 142. It bears the Minton mark and dates from the mid-1920s. Ht 6½in: 165mm.*

Colour Plate 163. *Lustreware is not something that one associates with Royal Worcester, but in the 1950s they produced a range of high-fired marked wares in silver lustre, of which this sucrier is an example. Ht 4¼in: 108mm.*

Colour Plate 164. *A fine example of the work of one of the leading artist potters, a tin-glazed bowl by Alan Caiger-Smith, with orange brushed lustre decoration. 1980.*

(The National Museums and Galleries of Merseyside, Liverpool Museum)

Appendix

Apart from those potteries, details of which are given in the preceding chapters, there were many others, particularly in Staffordshire, which contemporary writers such as Jewitt and documentary information from municipal records show were almost certainly producers of lustreware. Though not all of the early evidence can be relied on completely, more recent research has confirmed probably the majority of it, and there can be little doubt that a great deal of lustre was produced, sometimes by very small potteries indeed. A proviso here would be that a number of the firms may have had their actual lustring carried out by specialist decorating firms like Bailey and Batkin.

A very comprehensive survey of those potteries in which evidence of their lustreware rests primarily on the written word, appears in such publications as Rodney Hampson's *The Longton Potters* and in Gibson and Godden's *Collecting Lustreware*. But, among the potteries discussed, there are a certain number where a marked example of their work is also known to exist. As often or not this may be a single pot, but even such a small sample makes the names of the firms that produced them stand out from the rest.

A number of the potteries that fall into this category are named below and details given, either about where the marked ceramics may be seen, or of publications in which photographs of them appear.

Bailey & Harvey 1833-1835, Lane End. A picture of an impressed silver lustre cup and saucer and plate is in John and Baker's *English Lustre Pottery*.

Boardman c.1820. Possibly a Liverpool potter; possibly Staffordshire. Marked silver resist lustre jug pictured in *Collecting Lustreware*, p. 92.

Bott & Co. c.1807-1810, Lane End. Marked silver resist lustre bulb pot shown in *Collecting Lustreware*, p. 93.

Clews, R. & J. c.1815-1834, Cobridge. Lustre jug impressed 'Clews, Warranted Staffordshire' in Home Sweet Home Museum, East Hampton, NY.

Cork & Edge 1846-1860, Burslem. A marked lustre jug shown in Hugh Wakefield's *Victorian Pottery*.

Elliot, H. & Co. Newcastle. Marked and lustred children's plate with 'dancing dog' print shown in Noel Riley's *Gifts for Good Children*, p. 203.

Hilditch & Sons c.1819-1832, Lane End. For marked examples of silver lustre-decorated teawares see *Staffordshire Porcelain*, ed. Geoffrey Godden.

Mason, C.J. (& Co) c.1830-1834, Lane Delph (Staffs.). Two lustred Mason spill vases, Colour Plate 75.

Minton c.1796 to present day, Stoke. Marked silver resist lustre pottery teaset, Plate 142.

New Hall Company c.1782-1835, Shelton. Anthony de Saye Hutton's *A Guide to New Hall Patterns* shows four silver lustre designs.

Plant, B. 1784-1814, Lane End. A model lion incised 'B. Plant, Lane End', illustrated in *Collecting Lustreware*, has its paw resting on a silver lustre ball. From the Victoria and Albert Museum Collection.

Ridgway C. 1792 to present day. In the author's possession is a dish with a pattern in silver lustre which has been attributed to Ridgway.

Rivers, W. & Co. c.1816-1819, Shelton. The pink lustre plate in *Collecting Lustreware,* p. 149, is impressed 'Rivers'.

Rogers 1784-1842, Burslem. The large silver resist lustre dish from the City Museum and Art Gallery, Stoke, is impressed 'Rogers' (see *Collecting Lustreware,* p. 149).

Seaham Pottery 1836-1846, Seaham Harbour. A large Sunderland-style lustre jug with Seaham Pottery lettered under the spout is in the Sunderland Museum.

Stubbs, Joseph c.1822-1834. An impressed pink lustre plate is in the Roger T. Powers collection.

Warburton 1802-1823, Cobridge. An impressed silver resist plate was pictured in *The Connoisseur* for December 1907.

Wedg Wood, John 1841-1844, Burslem. Photographs of impressed teapot and coffee pot from the Geoffrey Fisk collection in *Northern Ceramic Society Journal,* Vol 6.

Weston, G. & Co. 1799-1829, Lane End. An impressed silver lustre jug is shown in *Collecting Lustreware,* p. 174.

Whitehaven Pottery, Cumbria (Harrison, Hall & Co.) c.1812-1816. An article by Elizabeth Adams in *Echoes and Reflections* (Northern Ceramic Society) includes quotes from a Whitehaven advertisement for 'Silver lustre teapots, sugar boxes and cream ewers'. Though no marked samples or photographs are known of the wares, it was felt important to record for this book that lustre was produced in Cumberland.

Bibliography

The following list is of titles, many of which are out of print, that should be of interest to the collector of lustreware. Comparatively few of them, however, have lustre as their main subject, but some are included to give an indication of wares that, in addition to a large or small range of lustred items, were produced by most of the factories. From a picture of a non-lustred jug or vase in one of these books it is sometimes possible to place a lustred item, the origin of which is in doubt, by comparing shapes or style of decoration with the possible maker. Some books include listings of manufacturers' marks. Unfortunately books, even among those dealing especially with lustred wares but particularly those dating from before about 1950, cannot by any means be relied on for accuracy. Several are little more than attractive picture books with captions which can only be described, in the kindest possible way, as fanciful. The authors have clearly repeated, without verification, erroneous information from other writers. Other books, probably wisely, make no attempt to link any item to a particular factory, but still have some interest, in that they give a collector an idea of how wide is the range of lustred pottery and porcelain available to them.

With the publication of John and Baker's very fully illustrated *Old English Lustre Pottery* in 1950, the picture began to change. Their work was the result of much careful study of their subject and for the first time a reasonably reliable guide to English (and Welsh) lustreware of the nineteenth century was available. Inevitably, since that time some of the authors' findings have been found not to be entirely accurate, but they had set a benchmark. The book is still one of the best guides available, only surpassed comparatively recently by Godden and Gibson's much more comprehensive *Collecting Lustreware*, which brings the story into the 1990s

Baker, John C. *Sunderland Pottery* (Tyne and Wear County Council Museums, Sunderland). 5th edition, 1984

Batkin, M. *Wedgwood Ceramics 1840-1959* (R. Dennis) 1982

Battie, D. and Turner, M. *The Price Guide to 19th and 20th Century British Pottery* (Antique Collectors' Club) 1979 with later editions

Bedford, J. *Old English Lustre Ware* (Cassell), 1965

Bell, R.C. *Tyneside Pottery* (Studio Vista) 1971

Bergesen, V. *Bergesen's Price Guide, British Ceramics* (Barrie & Jenkins) 1992

Berthoud, M. *H. and R. Daniel 1822-1846* (Micawber Publications) 1980

Blakey, H. and C. (ed.) *St Anthony's Pottery Newcastle upon Tyne* (Northern Ceramic Society and Tyne and Wear Museums) 1993

Caiger-Smith, A. *Lustre Pottery. Technique, Tradition and Innovation in Islam and The Western World* (Faber & Faber) 1985

Cameron, E. *Encyclopaedia of Pottery and Porcelain of the 19th and 20th Centuries* (Faber & Faber) 1986

Carter, P. *A Dictionary of British Studio Potters* (Scolar Press) 1990

Cross, A.J. *Pilkington's Royal Lancastrian Pottery* (R. Dennis) 1980

Des Fontaines, U. *Wedgwood Fairyland Lustre* (Sotheby Parke Bernet) 1975

Drakard, D. *Printed English Pottery 1760-1820* (Johnathan Horne) 1992

Feild, R. *Buying Antique Pottery and Porcelain* (Macdonald) 1987

Fleming, J.A. *Scottish Pottery* (Maclehose, Jackson & Co.) 1923

Gaunt, W. and Clayton-Stam, M.D.E. *William De Morgan* (Studio Vista) 1971

Gibson, M. *Lustreware,* (Shire Publications Ltd.) 1993

Godden, G.A. and Gibson, M. *Collecting Lustreware* (Barrie & Jenkins) 1991

Godden, G.A. *Encyclopaedia of British Pottery and Porcelain Marks* (Herbert Jenkins) 1963, many times revised and now Barrie & Jenkins

Godden, G.A., *British Pottery, An Illustrated Guide* (Barrie & Jenkins) 1974

Godden, G.A. *Encyclopaedia of British Porcelain Manufacturers* (Barrie & Jenkins) 1988

Halfpenny, P. (ed.) *Penny Plain and Twopence Coloured. Transfer Printing on English Ceramics 1750-1850* (The Potteries Museum, Hanley, Stoke-on-Trent) 1994

Henrywood, R.K. *Relief-Moulded Jugs 1820-1900* (Antique Collectors' Club) 1984

Hughes, G.B., *English and Scottish Earthenware 1660-1880* (Lutterworth Press) 1961

Jewitt, L. *The Ceramic Art of Great Britain* (Virtue & Co, two vols., 1878, revised, one vol. 1883)

John, W.D. and Warren Baker, Dr W., *Old English Lustre Pottery* (The Ceramic Book Company) 1951, 2nd edition 1962

Lewis, G., *A Collectors' History of English Pottery* (Studio Vista, 1969, 4th edition Antique Collectors' Club) 1999

Lockett, T.A. and Godden, G.A. *Davenport Pottery, Porcelain and Glass, 1794-1887* (Barrie & Jenkins) 1989

Lomax, A. *Royal Lancastrian Pottery, 1900-1908* (privately published) 1957

McVeigh, P. *Scottish East Coast Potteries, 1750-1840* (John Donald, Publishers Ltd.) 1979

Miller, J. J. *English Yellow-Glazed Earthenware* (Barrie & Jenkins) 1974

Moore, S. and Ross, C. *Maling, the Trademark of Excellence* (Tyne and Wear Museums Service) 1989

Nance, E. Morton. *The Pottery and Porcelain of Swansea and Nantgarw* (B.T. Batsford Ltd.) 1942

Niblett, P. and K. *Hand-Painted Gray's Pottery* (City Museum and Art Gallery, Stoke-on-Trent) 1982, revised editions 1983 and 1987

Pugh, R. *Welsh Pottery* (Towy Publishing) 1996

Reilly R. *Wedgwood* (Macmillan) 1989

Riley, N. *Gifts for Good Children – A History of Children's China 1790-1890* (Richard Dennis) 1991

Rudolph, W. *Sailor Souvenirs* (Edition Leipzig) 1998

Smith, A. *The Illustrated Guide to Liverpool Herculaneum Pottery* (Barrie & Jenkins) 1970

Warner, I. and Posgay, M. *The World of Wade* (Antique Publications, U.S.A.) 1988

Whiter, L. *Spode, A History of the Family, Factory and Wares 1733-1833* (Barrie & Jenkins) 1970, revised 1978, 1989

Williams-Wood, C., *English Transfer Printed Pottery and Porcelain* (Faber & Faber) 1981

Publications by Societies

Journal of Ceramic History (City Museum and Art Gallery, Stoke-on-Trent)

   Vol. 14 'Longton Potters' by Rodney Hampson

   Vol. 15 'Staffordshire Ceramics and the American Market 1775-1880' by Neil Ewins

Journal of the Northern Ceramic Society

   Vol 5 1984 'Thomas Lakin, Staffordshire Potter' by Harold Blakey

   Vol 5 1984 'John Wedg Wood of Bignall End' by Una Des Fontaines

   Vol 8 1991 'A London Staffordshire Warehouse' by A. Eatwell and A. Werner

   Vol 9 1992 'Sunderland Pottery' by N. Dolan

Scottish Pottery: 18th Historical Review 1996 (Scottish Pottery Society)

Index

Page numbers in bold type refer to illustrations and captions